Secret
Ceremonies

Secret Ceremonies

A Mormon Woman's

Intimate Diary of

Marriage and Beyond

Deborah Laake

William Morrow and Company, Inc.
New York

It is the policy of William Morrow and Company, Inc., and its imprints and affiliates, recognizing the importance of preserving what has been written, to print the books we publish on acid-free paper, and we exert our best efforts to that end.

Library of Congress Cataloging-in-Publication Data

Laake, Deborah.
    Secret ceremonies / by Deborah Laake.
        p.   cm.
    Includes index.
    ISBN 0-688-09304-3
    1. Laake, Deborah. 2. Ex-church members—Mormon Church—
Biography. 3. Women, Mormon—United States—Biography. 4. Mormon
Church—Controversial literature. I. Title.
BX8645.L22 1993
289.3'092—dc20
    [B]   92-40449
                                                                        CIP

Printed in the United States of America

4 5 6 7 8 9 10

BOOK DESIGN BY BARBARA COHEN ARONICA

This book is for B.,
whose generosity launched it.
It is also for Elisa Petrini,
who enlarged it.

This is a true story. However, to protect the privacy of some people I have known, I have changed their names, likenesses, and other identifying references. Only historical figures, family members, and a few on-the-record sources are still identifiable: myself, my relatives, Ernest Wilkinson, Ross Peterson, Joe Walker, and Karen Case. The names of those mentioned in the Introduction of the book and General Authorities of the Mormon Church who are quoted or referred to throughout the book are also real, but I have disguised the local bishops and others with whom I counseled directly.

Acknowledgments

A remarkable thing about this book is the way my mother and father have behaved about it. Although the Mormon Church is the center of their lives, although they have always known that my story about their church wouldn't please them, they have supported my telling it from the beginning. I am grateful to them for putting our relationship ahead of their beliefs.

I am also grateful to Michael Lacey, my friend and the executive editor of *New Times,* for never asking whether I was pulled in different directions by my job and the need to finish the manuscript. (I was.) He has championed this project in a way that editors used to, when writing in America still had status.

My agents, Gail Hochman and Marianne Merola, and their assistant, Heather Cristol, have loved this book and worked for it as though they'd written it. They have bucked me up and put me up.

The editing of *Secret Ceremonies* has been painful for nearly everyone involved; just as attachments were formed, the editors have moved on. Despite the unpredictable nature of New York publishing houses, however, I've been blessed with precisely the right overseer during crucial stages. Jim Landis believed in this project and bought it; Jane Meara provided insights for the first half of the manuscript, and her insights truly transformed the second; Bob Shuman took over during a difficult period and saw the manuscript through production with loving care. It is Elisa Petrini, however, whose presence is on every page. She understood where I was going even when I didn't, and she led me there with clearheaded comments and editing that have left me a better writer. She was my partner in this.

Very luckily, I belong to a community of writers who have provided unstinting help and encouragement whenever I've needed it. In particular, Ron Carlson critiqued much of the manuscript at a point where I'd bogged down, and he got me rolling again. Dewey Webb, the world's best headline writer, came up with the title. And Terry Greene and Kathleen Stanton, my partners in crime at the office, have endlessly sympathized with my discouragements and celebrated my breakthroughs.

I have also received inestimable help from a group of forthcoming Mormons who, although I was usually a stranger, agreed to tell me their private stories. Without their generosity and honesty, their willingness to poke around in often painful old memories, I'd have possessed no context for my own story as I unraveled it. Only a handful of them weren't hesitant for their names to appear in this book. My thanks to Phyllis Barber, Karen Case, Ellen Fagg, Carl Hunsaker, Gayle Kapaloski, Marian Merrill, Ross Peterson, Linda Sillitoe, and Paul Swenson. If we talked at length and your name isn't here, and you wouldn't have minded, it's only because I erred on the side of caution on your behalf.

Also in this group was Clare Goldsberry, to whom I owe special thanks. Not only were her memories of the temple ceremony more detailed than my own, but she was actually willing to share them. (As a rule, even the questioning and lapsed Mormons went mum when asked to describe this intricate ritual that's considered top secret.) The account contained here is as accurate as she and I, and the limited writings available, could make it.

I am also very grateful to Lavina Fielding Anderson for sharing with me her excellent paper on the history of dissidents and the church.

This brings me to my friends, who haven't let me quit when I've faltered and who do, in general, make my life worth living. Jane Aiken read early versions; Elaine Carlson couldn't hear enough; John Clark shared his memories; Heidi Ewart took up the slack so I could write; Thomas Hagerty sat through the entire last chapter as I read aloud; Scott Jacobson critiqued my proposal; Nancy Kitchell was always calling with ideas for the *next* book; Helen Sandalls and John Leshy loaned me the cabin when I needed to write in peace; Michael Schroeder was interested every day, and kept the dog; Lisa Smith has listened to me stutter and complain; Kevin Sullivan has tended the house when I'm away; and John Tandy painstakingly packed the car on a day when I was headed for the woods but neither of us believed I was well enough to write once I'd arrived. The other Elaine, who has known me during both my lives, has done research and provided housing. None of these services is the thing for which I thank them most, however: I thank them for everything they've taught me about commitment, and for loving me, so that my life is more solid than during the years this book describes.

Introduction

This book has taken a long time to write, primarily because I have kept losing my nerve. More than once I have stopped stone dead, unable for another moment to reveal such intimate acts in front of an audience I don't know.

But misgivings were temporary. I began to think this was a project worth the effort after a decade of telling the stories of my years as a young Mormon wife to close friends who then reacted with disbelief. If they were surprised by the innards of my early life—its marriages and divorces, secret ceremonies, wardrobe peculiarities and supernatural milestones—I was equally surprised by their ignorance of the aspects of Mormonism my anecdotes revealed. How was it possible, I wondered, that such informed people were continuing to take the church of my childhood at face value, as nothing more complex than a likable, family-oriented creed that embraces America's most wholesome and unambiguous values? For although Mormonism is benign and even steadying when viewed superficially, it has also long been providing to the world glimpses of the dark disturbances lying just beneath the surface.

How, I wondered, could the church's largely bland image have survived the memory of the murders committed in 1985 by Mark Hofmann, the Mormon master forger who, caught in the act of falsifying historical documents with which he intended to rewrite early Mormon church history, executed with homemade bombs those who he feared might expose him? Or Evan Mecham, an Arizona politician who claimed to have been called to his post by God but who, because he violated state campaign laws and possessed a heart filled with hate, became in 1988 the first U.S. governor to be impeached in nearly seventy years?

Or the murders within polygamous sects that are the offshoots of early Mormonism, most notably the slaying in 1977 of polygamous leader Rulon Allred by Ervil LeBaron, his rival?

Or the excommunication of Mormon housewife Sonia Johnson, a proceeding that in 1979 cracked open a door to reveal a tableau of patriarchy that we might otherwise have imagined doesn't exist in America?

Or the extremism of Bruce Longo, a former Mormon missionary and then a cult leader who believed he was God, who killed himself in 1978, and whose wife commanded their seven children to follow their father into the afterlife by jumping to their deaths from the eleventh story of a Salt Lake City hotel?

Or **John** Singer, the stubborn polygamist from Marion, Utah, who was shot down by law officers who insisted that his children attend public schools, and whose widow and son-in-law in 1988 commemorated the tenth anniversary of his death first by announcing that Singer would return from the grave to usher in the millennium, then by blowing up a Mormon chapel, and finally by transforming their farm into a firepowered fortress during a thirteen-day siege that ended with one policeman dead?

I understood that while these newsmakers weren't typical Mormons, their shocking stories weren't coincidences, either. Around the roots of all the lunacies were packed typical Mormon teachings, and one teaching in particular: that all Mormon men are "priesthood holders," anointed with the literal, supernatural, nearly unlimited authority to act for God on earth, and are headed into an eternal life where they will themselves become gods who rule entire worlds. It's a theological concept that, tucked into a brain that's egotistical or unbalanced, is a match to dynamite.

But it isn't widely known. Nor is much else that's fundamental to this metaphysical sect. As my friends reacted with astonishment to even my own stories of unimaginable rituals that had led straight to heartbreak when I was a young woman—quite an everyday version of Mormon life that would never make it into the papers—I saw clearly, for the first time, the extent to which the unnerving, mystical core of my native culture is still hidden, and I longed to bring into the light this piece of social history.

Mormonism is hidden despite a prominence that's startling. The Mormon Church is one of the world's most rapidly growing religions, with a membership of 8.2 million that is increasing at the rate of 300,000 a year because of its perfectly organized, worldwide missionary program that deploys 48,000 missionaries into more than one hundred countries. It is piloted by over one hundred middle-aged and elderly men who are its spiritual leaders, who are mostly white, and who are very often "called" to their honored positions out of business careers; in their hands, the church has grown into one of the most powerful economic institutions in the United States, with vast interests in retailing, broadcasting, insurance, and other areas; its real-estate holdings alone exceed $1 billion.

(Although the church leaders issue no financial reports, *The Arizona Republic* in 1991 undertook a lengthy investigation and estimated that the church's yearly income from members was $4.3 billion, with another $4 billion in sales streaming in from its business subsidiaries—figures that, if the church were a publicly traded company, would place it with Union Carbide and Borden Products on the *Fortune* 500 list.) It is a powerful political force in America when it mobilizes its members around an issue, as was true in the late seventies when priesthood leaders scrambled to help defeat the Equal Rights Amendment, and it holds particular sway throughout the American West, where its numbers are most concentrated. It is influential in every presidential administration, particularly when conservatives are in power. It is a rare religion that both started in America and is gaining in relevance here, as our society continues to be deeply divided between the Religious Right, of which Mormonism is a part, and everyone else.

And yet it is still a mystery.

These are political facts, but my book is personal, not political. It is about what happened when I was searching for young love. I have tried to illuminate the deeper nature of my heritage by telling my own story in detail, by struggling to cut close to the emotional bone for the truths that are hard to reach.

—D.L.

One

I

When I left home for college, I knew I was the sort of girl to whom romantic things had always happened and always would. In part, I knew it because I possessed good legs and lovely dresses, but I also could sense that the future would be perfect, which could mean only one thing. From the beginning I awakened in my dorm room with the feeling that the day ahead was made up only of opportunities for catching the glance of the love of my life as we passed each other on the sidewalk, and I fell asleep wondering how many more days would slide by before I found him. I knew that romance was about to overtake me.

This was my state of mind when I espied Robert Peck my first Sunday on campus, and he was never out of my heart after that.

I was drawn to him almost entirely because he was my Sunday-school teacher. I set a lot of store by his position, but I was also compelled by the extreme attitude of dignity with which he wore it. Even at age twenty-one, he was the sort of starchy fellow whom everyone called by both his names, always, as though the words were hyphenated. Robert-Peck. A nickname was unthinkable.

For what seemed like a very long time, our relationship

consisted only of the fact that every Sunday morning I watched his performance. His performance didn't vary much but I didn't mind, since in the years before I began to really know men I was able to think that Robert-Peck was perfect the way he was. Week after week, he strode to the front of the classroom, impeccable in a three-piece suit, glanced imperiously at the members of his audience and then rained down upon them a Niagara of theological theory such as was to be found only among the returned missionaries, the most assured members of the Brigham Young University campus where both Robert-Peck and I lived. He never actually reached for a watch fob at the conclusion of his lectures, but I always expected him to. What a prig he was. I loved him completely.

I think there's no real advantage to young love. On the Sunday morning when Robert-Peck finally approached me, I was so young that I thought the way I experienced myself was the way I appeared to others, and I couldn't imagine he'd be interested in a giggly and unfocused freshman. I wasn't old enough to know that controlling the spread of disbelief across my face might have provided me with a certain amount of emotional leverage. I think that as he loped over to me where I stood in the hallway of the stark school building that doubled as a Mormon chapel on weekends, I may actually have begun to inhale through my mouth.

"I thought we might do something after church," he said abruptly.

"All right," I said.

"I'll call you," he said, and loped away, taking with him my equilibrium.

I flew home ahead of nearly everyone. Flew to the dormitory compound, flew across the wedges of snow-covered lawn to my own building, flew up the stairs to my narrow room.

I remember how I flung myself facedown onto my bed and bit into my pillow to keep from crying out. And I know now that my excitement was not merely that of a young girl who has just been noticed by the object of her unbridled fantasies; it was a soul's keening when it feels itself to be on the verge of spiritual fulfillment. I felt that I'd been called by the Lord.

It was easy for me to confuse the Lord's voice with Robert's: That is how much I admired an outstanding man. I also, at age eighteen, already desperately wanted to marry one, since I knew that my success in this life and the next was dependent upon it. The importance of such a marriage was the primary lesson of my Mormon girlhood, when it had been repeatedly impressed upon me that if I failed to marry a faithful Mormon man in a ceremony performed in a Mormon temple, I would be denied access to the highest level of Mormon heaven. Mormon heaven is very complicated: It is made up of three graduated "kingdoms," but only the uppermost tier—the Celestial Kingdom—has any real status. And I had never intended to miss it.

But I had never dreamed that I might become acquainted with it in the company of someone like Robert-Peck, either, who seemed to me to be a religious giant of a man because of the eloquence of his Sunday-school lessons. I had never dreamed it because no man of spiritual distinction had ever shown a fleck of interest in me before.

Before the other girls returned from church and crowded chattering onto the floor, I tried to figure out why I had always been ignored by the young men I knew who struck me as being close to God. The only conclusion I came to was that I didn't show well, spiritually speaking. Where in Book of Mormon class some coeds were moved to raise their hands and make scriptural references, I raised my hand and made jokes.

Where some girls yearned to become the head of the women's auxiliary in our congregations, which the Mormons call "wards," I didn't want to be distracted by church responsibilities from the time-consuming pleasures of floating from one college party to another. I was content to lead the music at the evening service.

And yet I knew I was not unpious. I felt my fierce commitment to Mormonism beating within me every day that I climbed up the slope from Helaman Halls to the modern, splayed-out buildings of the main campus. I would watch a mob of Mormon students flowing along to classes as unanimously as though they were parts on the same car, rarely trespassing onto the grass because it was against the rules, and I would think I had seen a vision of the kingdom of God. When I crammed for my Book of Mormon finals, staying up through exam week's eternal nights, the mornings found me still bent over the book of scripture and close to tears with my growing conviction that I was reading revealed truths.

And nearly always, I felt God's presence within me like a warm thumb pressing on my heart. It had always been true, but it was particularly true once I reached Utah, the center of the Mormon universe and the holy land I'd longed to tread all my life.

How I wanted to come together with a man of such instinctive spiritual gifts that he would recognize the unobvious depths of my love for worship. As my floormates were coming up the stairway two and three at the time, I was flinging shirts and skirts and slacks onto my bed, rummaging for the combination that would impress Robert-Peck.

The phone rang before I was dressed, and his voice leaped through the line with a commanding tone and a plan that I have remembered exactly for twenty years. "I have some milk, and I have some cookies in a bag, and I am coming around to see you," he said.

It was a very clear winter day and the sun was melting a recent storm into mush, so Robert-Peck and I wound up sloshing our way to the old portion of upper campus. We did not exactly move as a team. I got the feeling that Robert, clutching his bag of provisions, was still tuned in to the full-speed-ahead rhythms he'd learned while proselytizing door to door on his two-year mission to England. He hadn't been back in the States very long, and like many returned Mormon missionaries, he was still more accustomed to walking with a silent male missionary companion than with a girl intent on talk. While he raced ahead I padded after him, deluging his back with cheerful conversational gambits like a servant throwing rose petals after the master.

We finally came to a circle of trees that sheltered some benches set into a little hollow. It was there we consumed our simple repast, swigging milk from the same carton, and began also to consume each other's eyes. Whatever my spiritual shortcomings, I was a girl who took some pleasure in the world, who let fly often with a raucous laugh, and Robert was gazing at me like a parched bush that has spotted a watering can. As my flirting progressed, his stern, handsome face actually crinkled and softened with amusement several times. Before too long he'd taken my hand and begun to lead me back down the hill.

We wandered, I think unconsciously, toward the Smith Fieldhouse. It was a vast and echoing arena that could probably hold the majority of the student body and that never came completely alive, not even during the concert appearances of Bread and John Denver and other watered-down rock stars whom stodgy church leaders were willing to allow on campus.

On this Sunday afternoon, it was unlocked and empty and dark.

Robert-Peck began to speak from his heart as we neared it. The last of his formality fell away and he seemed like just a very young man out walking with a girl. "The thing I want is to see God in this life," he said with great earnestness. "To see Him just the way I'm seeing you. I think He will show himself eventually if I live close enough to Him every day. So it's very important that I keep myself righteous."

I did not think this was strange—although I did think it was extreme—because at BYU the concern with God permeated everything, particularly courtship. It was not uncommon for coeds to whisper a quick prayer before going to meet their dates, or for the men to suggest to first dates, once everybody was settled in the car, that they pray together for the spirit of the Lord to protect them from committing any unchaste acts during the course of the evening. ("Please, please, *please* let him like me!" was the form my own prayers took when I knew somebody was waiting in the lobby. But I offered them every time and on my knees.)

I particularly did not think it was strange that attaining perfect faith seemed vital to Robert-Peck, because I expected spiritual dedication from a member of the Mormon priesthood. All Mormon men are ordained to the priesthood—a designation that they believe has been passed down to them directly from Christ's apostles, one that endows them with mystical and supernatural powers, such as the ability to perform miraculous healings and exorcisms. They also believe that their priesthood powers carry grave responsibilities for righteous living.

I saw Robert-Peck framed in the last sun, looking as strong and sacrosanct as Jesus. And because I couldn't distinguish between young romance and the urgent emotions of the spiritual haze engulfing us, I believed I was fated for this young man with whom I'd just spent my first hours.

Still, I'm sure neither of us really expected that we were going to climb into the lightless bleachers and fall into each other's arms. Ours was a culture where people our age still spent a lot of time weighing whether to kiss on first dates. (Kiss once, at the end.) I have come to suspect in the years since it happened that when he pulled me toward him and bent to cover my lips and face with kisses, that it was unreal to him, that some part of him was watching us from a distance, astonished at the acts of unguarded passion that he'd never unleashed before in his life.

But whatever his feelings were, they couldn't have been more life-changing than mine. In the hour of soft sounds before we walked slowly back to the dorm, I became a fulfilled woman. For the first and last time, I experienced my life working out exactly as my parents and church leaders had told me since birth that it would. I was in Utah at last, and I was pressing every allowable part of my body against the chest and cheeks of a man whose skin made my own skin hum, and who, wonder of wonders, was that elusive thing, "spiritual." And he was taking me seriously.

I finally belonged.

II

While I was growing up it had seemed that I would always be outside life's window because I was religious. In the late sixties, my classmates at my Florida high school were the younger siblings of the chanting, swaying, agonized college insurrectionaries whose activism was transforming the country, and I—who poured all my own passion into following as exactly as I could a path paved with endless "church standards" for behavior—couldn't begin to understand or approve of them.

During the final weeks before graduation, when black armbands commemorating the recent killings at Kent State were wound as purposefully as tourniquets around my classmates' biceps and the school flew apart with song-filled sit-ins in the corridors, I went along placidly to classes. When my peers erupted with particular gusto by smashing their framed awards at the annual dean's list banquet, I pursed my lips at the unnecessary way they'd insisted on ruining a lovely occasion.

I had spent those tumultuous years waiting for a more suitable context, huddled for companionship with the other Mormon teenagers I knew, which was not a vast or varied group in our corner of the South. My siege of waiting had ended only in the fall of 1970, a few months before Robert-Peck took me to the field house, when I had rolled triumphantly onto the BYU campus in my father's barge of a car.

By then my former schoolmates had meandered off to their own institutes of higher learning clutching a few pairs of bellbottom jeans and perhaps some moccasins. As for me, I was surrounded in Dad's backseat by sweater boxes and department-store hangers sheathed with knotted plastic bags. Except for the narrow slash of upholstery where I had staked out a slight territory for my person, the entire rear compartment and even the window ledge were filled with the winter wardrobe that my mother and I had just spent an entire week collecting in Salt Lake City's most elegant emporiums. There was not a pair of blue jeans in the lot.

This was because BYU, church-owned and archconservative, was not somewhere jeans were admired or even allowed. During a year when short hemlines were so accepted nationally that they'd become a uniform, BYU's strict dress code still forbade miniskirts anywhere on campus and mandated that young women could not wear slacks of any kind to classes. Such restrictions on personal expression might have caused revolution among college radicals, but as my parents and I motored toward my dormitory, I was unruffled by any stirrings of individualism or social conscience. The traditions of my religion had mainly taught me to be concerned with my suitability for wifehood, so that the emotional high point of my life until then had been my anxiety to page dreamily through *Vogue* pattern books of dresses for brides.

Which isn't to say that I was a placid girl. I was tingling past my fingertips while my father was lugging all those boxes up the stairway to my room in William Budge Hall; my heart was sure that by arriving at this sloping, status-quo campus in the city nicknamed Happy Valley I had at last hit the bull's-eye. And my mind's eye was imagining me in my many ensembles, chatting and dancing my way through a variety of college gatherings.

On the morning when I strolled on pristine walkways over to the field house and the welcoming assembly, I was so empty of meaningful ambition that I didn't bother to carry with me the books I needed for the long day's load of classes. I could hardly believe the sight that greeted me that day. After years of living among hippies-in-embryo while personally maintaining the grooming standards of an airline stewardess,

I had now found 25,000 soulmates. I could not gaze enough
at the hordes of college kids milling around me in their bright,
neat sweaters and pressed skirts and slacks and well-polished
shoes. I fell slightly in love with most of the young men I
espied because they were brutally barbered and clean-shaven—
it was the rule of the school. As for the coeds, they clustered
together in the fall sunlight, their masses of long hair so
obsessively shampooed that the sheen was incandescent. And
in an era when much of the university-aged world had embraced a concept of beauty that relied on the mixed blessings
of nature, my new sisters and I were swabbed with a quantity
of makeup that would have camouflaged burn victims.

When my high school counselor had summoned me to
his office a year earlier, and had thrown down before me with
a flourish the results of college entrance exams he said would
guarantee my admission to many of the best universities in
America, I had pushed the paper back in his direction as
nonchalantly as though I were passing him a napkin. "I'm a
Mormon," I had told him with a complacency that didn't
invite discussion. "I'm going to Brigham Young." That first
day at BYU, as I scanned the bleachers for a seat, I was a girl
capable of perfect decisions.

We were to be welcomed that morning by Ernest Wilkinson, the long-term, practically mythical president of BYU. He
was a man of seventy, a squat, workaholic attorney of distin-
guished reputation, who at the pinnacle of his law career had
represented many Indian tribes in their suits against the feds,
obtaining the largest settlement for the Utes—$25 million—that
had ever been squeezed out of the U.S. government. At the
university where he had ruled for twenty years, he was notoriously authoritarian, a powerful-voiced despot with the unfor-

tunate manner of a pit bull, given to ferocious public attacks on the phenomenon of campus disturbances. In 1966 he'd set the tone for compliance by advising parents and students that enrollment at BYU was a "privilege and not a right," and in 1968, at the height of the country's spasms of campus violence, he'd barked this at incoming freshmen: "In my judgment, students who would destroy the educational institutions which their fathers and mothers and the American people have provided for them should be deprived of their American citizenship and should hereafter, like Philip Nolan, be men without a country."

It says something about my own belief in obedience that these remarks had not seemed excessive. On the contrary, I'd been impressed, and was doubly thrilled when I'd heard that Wilkinson's sentiments had been greeted with resounding applause from the members of his young audience. I had come to my own freshman assembly hoping to be similarly inspired.

And Wilkinson did not disappoint: Again he began to pontificate passionately about the war that was tearing America apart. "We do not, at this institution, advise you how you can evade the draft—we teach you here how to serve your country," he said. . . . "We would sooner pay the supreme sacrifice on the field of battle and have our liberty than be at peace as abject slaves. We therefore have no sympathy with those who say that the war in Vietnam is immoral and unjust. The facts are that that war is just as 'moral and just' as any war in which we have engaged. They have all proceeded on the altar of freedom."

As his magnified voice zoomed into the highest eaves of the field house, followed by the roar from an ocean of students erupting in applause, I wasn't a bit aware that Wilkinson and his fans were acting out an irony. But if I'd pondered it, I'd have realized that I'd never personally met a Mormon teenager who went to war. Nor would I.

I know that there were Mormon soldiers in Vietnam because Wilkinson spoke that day of BYU students who had served. But the boys I knew at BYU enjoyed more security from the draft than other college students; I never once saw the shadow of anticipated death darken a discussion between them as they loitered in hallways or over hamburgers. Not only were they eligible for student deferments, but they could easily extend their years of safety by going on missions, a two-year activity that occurred in the middle of their college years and that exempted them from military service because they were ministers. (Even nonstudents could opt for missions.) When they returned to school from their missions, their student deferments were typically reinstated, and by graduation they had often rendered themselves ineligible by marrying young and having immediate babies, in the Mormon tradition.

Even as Wilkinson's warmongering was washing over me, my brother Len, whose lottery number was 51, was proselytizing in Germany on the second leg of this program. He hadn't gone there specifically to avoid the draft, and yet my parents and I were grateful and relieved he had avoided it. There must have been a lot of similar emotions behind the bravos of Wilkinson's student body that morning.

I don't think those cheering children were hypocrites, though. For one thing, patriotism is important to Mormons, often in a fierce and unexamined way. I imagine that when their legitimate excuses were exhausted, more young Mormon men filed meekly into transport planes than fled to Canada or consumed countless egg whites in an attempt to elevate the

level of albumin in their urine. And I also suspect that a lot of
the kids in that auditorium were thrilling less to Wilkinson's
sentiments than to the cozy sense of his power over their lives.

For that is what finally overtook me as the old man's
remarks worked their tiny teeth within me. He moved past his
concern with Vietnam and began to address the code of student behavior, weaving back and forth between weighty issues
of moral turpitude and truly eccentric insistences. As he spoke,
I found my breast filling with devotion to my new leader in
the same unthinking way that I had already loved a long line
of local church elders since my birth.

*"It is expected of you that you . . . will greet each other as you
see each other on campus,"* he told us.

*"The tradition on this campus . . . is to attend church on Sunday.
. . . I hope that this hint will be sufficient, for we have at this university
exit as well as admission standards."*

The list went on and on, mowing down before it every
possible shoot of bad behavior that might thrust like a weed
through the surface of Ernest Wilkinson's world. And since
recognizing and supporting authority is one of the church's
major tenets, I began to buzz with the pleasant prospect of
backing up my president's nitpicking program with my dedication to it.

*"We should avoid speeding. . . . We should always have our seat
belts on."*

*". . . We do not leave any meeting before the end of the
meeting."*

I had strolled over to this assembly accompanied by a
newfound friend who was also a floormate. Now I found
myself reaching for her hand and anchoring myself with it. I
wanted to be part of her and of everyone else in that pretty
audience. I found myself thinking that we all fit together like

gear components, so that the machine of our marvelous school could run.

"*. . . We should report any wrongdoing on this campus. Otherwise we are not our brother's keeper.*"

I glanced over at my friend and vowed silently to protect her.

"*I should therefore like at this time to know, by rising vote, how many of you students are willing to uphold the standards of this institution by observing them yourselves and by seeing that others do also,*" Wilkinson was saying.

I tried to be one of the first on my feet.

III

From the beginning of our courtship, I expected that Robert-Peck and I would get married. I soon came to believe that he loved me, and more important, I figured I was living in a manner that guaranteed I would have my way:

My ideas about husbands and wives and God were the exact ones I'd learned in Sunday school as a child.

I was obeying a staggering number of "commandments" that the church leaders kept harping on.

In particular, I was remaining as chaste as a plant, despite my passion for Robert.

I knew it was a winning formula, since I had always been taught that obedience was very exactly rewarded. Sunday after Sunday, the members of my home congregations had jumped to their feet to exclaim tearfully how they had received an unexpected cash windfall because they had paid a full tithe to the church. Or that because they'd been holding regular family prayer their luggage had been recovered safely after the chaotic flight out of Atlanta. I knew how to make life work out.

And anyway, I thought Robert and I were meant to be together. As winter warmed into spring, nothing mattered to the two of us beyond finding each other at the end of the day and leaving each other at the last moment before the dorms closed, and I began to love him for the boyish qualities that were uncovered during moments when his stuffiness simmered down. I stood at my window one weekend afternoon and watched him lope across the lawn between our dorms, running with a body gone floppy with infatuation and release. At one point he stopped to scoop up snow in his gloved hands and hurl a snowball uncontrolled into the sky. And there was a Saturday night when he came by for me late and we ended up somehow at a nearby baseball diamond where, at eleven P.M. in the pitch dark, we staged an entire baseball game without a bat or a ball. "It's a double!" I would scream to him when I was at the plate, and he would tear into the outfield, his arm stretched to the ground as though to intercept my hit. He got it sometimes; he missed it sometimes.

But his outflung attitude didn't last, and perhaps it couldn't have. He was not a man able to give in to the lunacies of love. Soon I was forced to notice his discomfort with his new demonstrative ways.

We were on our way to a devotional assembly the first time he mentioned the problem. I looked forward extravagantly to devotionals, which were weekly occasions when the bowling alley and the library and other outposts of idling were shut down so that students would not be tempted to stay away. Once gathered inside the field house, we were held captive by the highest leaders of the church. Called General Authorities, these windy men descended upon us one at a time from Salt Lake City sixty miles north to exhort us to be prayerful, to be grateful, to be virgins. Their middle-aged voices rose and fell with simplistic and singsong sentiments. "You *beautiful* young people, how *beloved* you are in our *hearts*" was the sort of thing they would intone. "How we *encourage* you to *continue* to keep your standards *high.*"

I loved these assemblies because I didn't have to pay any real attention to them. Their purpose lay as completely in the hypnotic waves of sound washing over me, reassuring and claiming me, as in anything that was actually said. So I could sit possessively by Robert, who often became quite absorbed in the rhetoric, and break his concentration occasionally by slipping my hand into his. Devotionals were opportunities for me to stake my claim on him in public.

I was feeling very eager and unsuspecting on that brilliant morning when my solemn suitor first began to share what was troubling him, and at first I didn't absorb what he was saying because I was distracted by the waves in his beautiful dark hair. I was still reveling in just looking at Robert-Peck.

He said, "I am focusing too much time on you."

"How is that possible?" I wanted to know, once his statement had sunk in. From my end I couldn't imagine such a thing.

"It's possible because you're not all my life is about. My life is about living close to God," he told me. I could see the old pomposity coming into him, straightening his spine and stiffening his walk a little. He let go of my hand, and my hand began to throb.

He went on, "My ambition is to live so close to God that He will reveal *everything* about my life to me. I see no reason why, if I'm completely in tune with Him, He won't tell me what time it's best to get up in the morning and what I should have for breakfast. And that kind of dedication requires a lot of attention."

"Why would God care what you have for breakfast?" I asked belligerently, startled at my own outburst. Always before, I had respected Robert's standing as a priesthood holder too much to challenge his beliefs, even to myself.

This is not to say that I'd ever given him the impression I was a genuinely reverent girl. "I have known you would feel that way," he said, his voice distant. "You don't want to be with Him as much as I do. Deborah, sometimes I don't think you're spiritual enough for me."

He may have said more or less than that, but his condemnation of my most vulnerable traits is what I remember. As I sat beside him at the field-house assembly I never found the courage to reach out for his hand, and when we parted on the sidewalk afterward, I felt too ashamed to raise my face for a kiss. I was a little young to be running up against the breed of man who will set his woman completely aside because he's got work to do, so I felt cut off from Robert-Peck by my unworthiness. I believed that because of his "priesthood" and the pipeline it gave him to God, he probably knew who and what I was.

IV

For the next few days I slunk around the campus semi-avoiding Robert. I missed him, but I hated myself too much to feel that I deserved to be with him. And that's where things stood toward the end of the week when, sitting with my scriptures open and my instructor's voice thrumming the verses in Book of Mormon class, I nearly found my feet again.

The Book of Mormon purports to be a history of the American Indians, and we were studying the book of III Nephi, wherein the ancient Indians were visited by Christ. I was not a fan of scripture's archaic language and had always put off scripture study, but while in the library with Robert-Peck only the week before, I had managed to read III Nephi for the first time. I hadn't liked it: The vast crowds of Indians dropping to their knees before Christ, weeping and praying aloud, had struck me as silly and overdone. Beneath my boyfriend's reproving stare, I'd been unable to keep from giggling and occasionally hissing a verse aloud for effect.

But that day in class, my religion professor, Brother Morton, intoned a passage where Christ is moved by the love being shown him by the crowds. He calls out to them, "My bowels are filled with compassion towards you! My bowels are filled with mercy!" Brother Morton was a spindly man with huge eyeglasses and tiny eyes that even thick lenses couldn't seem to magnify; when he read aloud his voice was thin and high. Yet in that moment I was overwhelmed, my imagination inflamed with the spectacle of Christ and the Indians, with the miracle of Christ's love emanating from his very bowels. Suddenly my chest opened up and I realized I was weeping.

I was sure that *I* couldn't be the fount of so much feeling; only God had that kind of power. I was sure that I was communicating directly with God! It was hard in that moment to know whether the more distracting rush was the message from heaven itself or the strength of my relief. Whatever Robert-Peck had said, I remembered now that I wasn't spiritually hopeless, because God had always considered me worth touching. Throughout my life, I'd been hearing from Him during moments like these.

I'd been blessed by Mormonism with a friendly God who insinuated Himself into my heart that way, bringing comfort and insight and understanding of hurt, and I had always sought to draw close to Him because I knew who He was very particularly. According to Mormon doctrine, He was an exalted, resurrected man who had performed especially well as a human and had earned as His reward the right to rule a slew of planets. He was not an exclusive God—there were infinite planets, and an infinite number of Gods controlling them—but He was my God and He cared about every aspect of my life, especially as long as I was making an effort to please Him. He was also slightly prone to personal appearances: When Joseph Smith, the founding prophet of Mormonism, was only fourteen, he saw God descend out of heaven with His son, Jesus, beside Him.

That morning in 1823 marked the beginning of Mormonism and an occasion when God had stayed awhile to converse. He was not always capable of providing hands-on attention, however, so, according to Smith's accounts, was greatly aided in His work by a cavalcade of spirits swooping constantly into the lives of mortals to advise or interfere or cajole. For instance, the Angel Moroni—once an early inhabitant of the American continent—also appeared to Smith in order to deliver a set of ancient gold tablets, the most primitive history of the American Indians, which the young prophet then translated into the Book of Mormon. (The Book of Mormon is considered by Mormons to be a corollary to the Bible, which they also believe to be scripture although they take the Book of Mormon more to heart. They think that Smith's translation is very pure.)

Smith is best known to the outside world for the Book of Mormon and for his radical preference for plural marriage, but those accomplishments constitute just a sliver of his influence within the church. In the fourteen years he stood at its head, he occupied himself with various aspects of religious sorcery, performing miraculous healings and receiving from God an endless stream of "revelations" designed to help mankind navigate the walk through life. These last became a bedrock of Mormon scripture.

An extraordinary number of Smith's revelations concerned spiritualism. When he died, shot out of an upstairs window by a member of an Illinois mob, he left behind the doctrine that every member of his church was surrounded by fabulous ghosts—the glorious dead, the wistful unborn, the searching and the monstrous—as well as an understanding that every man and woman was entitled to hear from ghosts, and from God, as routinely as in later years modern Mormons would pick up the phone.

Since babyhood, when my parents had first begun passing Smith's wisdom on to me, I'd been instructed in how to discern the difference between a messenger from God and one from the devil, whenever spirits appeared to me. On another occasion I'd been told solemnly, as though it mattered a great deal, that angels do not have wings. I'd had it explained to me why evil spirits walk around among us (they want to claim our bodies as their own) and what the scope of their power is (they must yield the floor when in the presence of godly spirits).

I believed I needed all this information, because ghosts did appear in our family's everyday lives occasionally. One morning my mother entered her bedroom and found Uncle Howard sitting on her bed, although Uncle Howard had been dead for twenty years. He was visiting out of concern for his son, who was not showing an outstanding interest in church attendance; he hoped that Mother would talk to the boy. Mother said Howard looked just the same as when he had died in a plane crash right at the end of the war.

When I was eleven and my grandmother died, my mother told me that Grandma was in the room with us, with her hands laid on my mother's head. I imagined that Grandma had been allowed by God to stop off and say good-bye.

These stories and Smith's were only the beginning of my faith in figments. In the atmosphere of undiluted faith at BYU, my greatest influence became the faculty members and their folklore. My professors specialized in spiritual folklore, though I couldn't have called it "folklore" then. I heard many mystical stories personally from my teachers, but I remember most clearly a story told me by my brother Len, who began attending BYU during my sophomore year, when he'd completed his mission. Len said that his religion professor, one of the most highly respected men of God on campus, had quieted a student's challenge on a point of theology with an unbrookable argument, saying, "I don't understand how what you are saying can be true. If it were true, I never would have been able to pass through the veil and see the afterlife. And I have."

We students were not far behind our teachers in the rush to expose our spiritual credentials. We told "faith-promoting" stories constantly, to impress our friends and to teach each other how to behave. The one that affected me the most as a freshman had to do with a student whose date had attacked her in the car. In the middle of the struggle, the coed had the astonishing presence of mind to speak the words her parents had taught her as a rebuke against evil. Desperately laying her hand against the would-be rapist's forehead, she told him, "In the name of Jesus Christ, I command you to leave me alone." And an invisible power lifted the bounder off her and pinned him, paralyzed, up against the driver's door.

I was thrilled and terrified by this story, but the thrill was the bigger part. I heard it many times; the legend blew through the campus and kept finding its way into women's auxiliary meetings. The first time I heard it, though, I was sitting with a group of dorm mates at dinner, and for a few moments everything in the cafeteria seemed to have stopped moving; the students still winding through the food line froze into snapshots. I was filled to capacity with sharp imaginings of the perfect faith of the girl in the story, and I longed to live the rest of my life very deeply and in tune with God.

There were other forms of spiritual life available to me at BYU besides fantastic tales. I frequently gathered for conventional prayers with the girls on my floor; I engaged in quiet talk with schoolmates out on the dormitory lawn, and we talked about the Bible.

It's just that the folklore, because it was so stirring, was for me always the heart. The miracles that lived in my imagination convinced me that Mormons were especially valued by God, and gave me the confidence to draw close to Him.

It was these many moments of intimacy that I remembered as I sat in front of Brother Morton. I wasn't able to hold on to the memories, but for a few minutes I was more in touch with all I was than with Robert-Peck's accusations.

V

Robert-Peck and I went on seeing each other, but it was never the same. He began calling less frequently; the phone would be silent for a day, and then two days, as though he had put himself on a weaning schedule. The days when I didn't hear from him became blank shafts of time when I hardly knew that I was going to classes or down to the cafeteria for dinner. The only activity I was aware of was the waiting. Then on the weekends, the terrible tension would flow out of my body for a few hours while we sat clasping hands in the close campus theaters where we could catch a second-rate flick for a dollar.

Afterward, we didn't go to the deserted Smith Fieldhouse anymore. Robert took me home early and pecked at my lips with only slight affection. From my dorm window, I would watch his back moving away from me until it disappeared into the dark. His posture was always ramrod straight. Even from a distance, his dignity was chilling.

He began to dislike the qualities in me that he'd most enjoyed. Where he had loved my loud laugh, the sound of it now flooded his face with impatience and a little pain, as though he felt a headache coming on.

Where he'd loved my long legs and way with clothes, he couldn't disapprove enough of the fact that I was called up before the BYU standards board to answer for my growing collection of miniskirts. His shock was so complete that it was as though he'd never seen my dresses before, as though they'd become short overnight.

Where he'd once liked the fact that I would occasionally skip out on a women's auxiliary meeting in order to have time to myself outdoors, he now began to wish I would take my responsibilities to the church more seriously.

And on a Sunday when he surprised me by showing up at my door on the one day a month men were allowed into the dorms, there was no mistaking his displeasure when he saw that he'd awakened me. Once he had actually reveled in the fact that I often fell intensely asleep in the middle of the day; he'd exclaimed that I went at my life with so much energy that I used myself up, the way a toddler falls facedown into a nap while playing. Now he took in the way my eyes were still struggling with the light and the fact that the rest of me was only barely clad in a nightgown as skimpy as anything Cher has ever worn to an awards ceremony, and his expression was forbidding. "I'll come back when you're yourself, and dressed," he said. His gorgeous eyes refused to linger for even one long look.

During that painful spring, I began to realize that I was vivid, and that vividness was not an attractive thing in a woman. I began to see that it was hard to be vivid without breaking all the rules.

Finally, when school was nearly over, I made one slight attempt to defend myself.

"I think I have it in me to be a spiritual leader in the ward," I remember telling him one Sunday while we were on our way in the near-dark to the evening service. "I just haven't applied myself in that direction."

He didn't reply right away, but though we had been strolling with our hands entwined, he released me, walking with his hands clasped behind his back. After a little silence he said encouragingly, "I'm sure you could do it." And then later, sharply, as though reading my mind, "You always want to *touch* so much."

VI

As the years have passed it has occurred to me that Robert-Peck was nothing more exaggerated than a returned missionary. Like so many of the young men who had dedicated two years of their lives to proselytizing, he had become so weighed down with his godly responsibilities that he had missed his youth. All my life I had been watching the boys I knew best play out the same process, but only at BYU did I begin to recognize the liabilities.

One friend of mine, a pretty girl with a hot attitude who was also a freshman, once went to kiss an RM only to have him push her indignantly away. "Do you think you could qualify to get into the temple?" he asked her. In order to enter a Mormon temple, you must submit yourself to a list of questions designed to weed out the unworthy, and some of the questions are about sex. None of the questions is about kissing, though. The RM just got carried away.

Not all the boys were like that. Some of them were just the opposite. After two years without women, they couldn't get enough of anything the BYU coeds were willing to provide—which I suspect was often not much. Either way, RMs could be extreme, and not just about sex, either.

They couldn't really help it, because their training was extreme: All their lives, they were schooled in the greatness of their own power. They knew they would "hold the priesthood" once they were twelve, and that the Mormon priesthood meant more than a starched collar—it meant the literal power to act for God. Priesthood transformed the boys I knew into supernatural beings, forever able to heal their children's fevers in the middle of the night or to cast devils out of their wives, and it guaranteed them positions as the "head of the house." A lesson manual for fourteen-year-old boys explained the entitlement this way: "The patriarchal order is of divine origin and will continue throughout time and eternity. There is, then, a reason why men, women and children should understand this order and this authority in the households of the people of God. . . . It is not merely a question of who is perhaps best qualified. Neither is it wholly a question of who is living the most worthy life. It is a question largely of law and order."

It was impossible to avoid an awareness of the possibilities. Every Sunday throughout their lives, young men filed into men-only classes, called priesthood meetings, where they learned they would become gods in the next life, capable of creating and ruling their own worlds. This major tenet of Mormonism came from the writings of Joseph Smith, writings that the Mormons consider scripture. To be fair, young Mormon women were also taught they could become goddesses. We were not instructed that our primary responsibility as goddesses would be government, however. We were told we would bear our husbands' "spirit children" throughout eternity.

When they turned nineteen, young Mormon men marched out of their priesthood meetings and into the mission field, into a kind of service without corollary in the modern world. They were encouraged as missionaries to give full vent to their mystical powers, which came to them in the form of hunches or whisperings, in order to locate the most receptive converts or to know the precisely inspiring thing to say to a reluctant one. A friend of mine from Florida—a gentlemanly, deliberate fellow whose mission took him to Mexico—actually cast a devil out of a woman on a street in Guadalajara. The boys began to believe that God was keeping a close watch over them and would inspire them in their smallest actions.

In areas where church members were sparse, the missionaries became the leaders of their wards, and at the age of nineteen or twenty they began counseling the other members of the congregation and exercising authority over their lives.

If his two years in the mission field ignited and fanned a man's belief in his mystic ways, once he arrived at BYU he had the opportunity to set himself ragingly ablaze. For there he was greatly admired, and slid into the same cloud of classes and spiritual stories that had immediately engulfed me. You heard about things happening among the men, amazing things, such as the time my friend Jacob actually heard God's voice.

He had been assigned to minister to two dozen freshmen boys, whom he taught, counseled, and came to love. One morning as he knelt with them and led them in prayer, as he saw that their neatly trimmed heads were expectantly bent, he was overcome with what he felt was the spirit of God actually speaking into his mind. The words were no longer his.

"I the Lord love you and forgive you of your sins," he heard himself saying. "You mustn't be afraid to come unto Me. If you open your hearts, My voice is always with you." It went on like that, in the first person, the words rushing into a room quivering with increasing power and surprise. Went on until all the words ran out. When Jacob finally finished, he could see that his boys were gripped by the same sense of might that he was feeling.

Later in the day he came upon his students where they had all gathered in a room; they were murmuring gravely with their chairs pulled very close together. As he came toward them they rose in one instinctive movement, as though they were greeting Christ. He was twenty-four. It was very heady stuff for a boy.

VII

Once Robert-Peck had succumbed to missionary propriety, I saw the boy of the baseball diamond only once more, and only for a moment.

We were separated for the summer, an endless season that I spent in Provo while he returned to California. I should have had a marvelous time without him: I was an editor on the school paper and was surrounded by cheerful girlfriends and would-be beaux. I also was mobile for the first time, since my father had just presented me with a sleek sports car that was the color of a green apple. Once I took it out on the highway between Provo and Salt Lake City and pushed it to 110, and it seemed that the wind would strip my hair off.

But that was a rare moment of exhilaration. For the most part I brooded and waited for Robert-Peck's letters, which were painfully restrained. Although I was barely into my sophomore year, he pushed me to consider graduate school; he also sent me an article from *Atlantic Monthly*. I found the letters very discouraging, since they had to do only with my mind. I suspected that Robert-Peck had quit thinking about my body altogether.

Whatever my doubts were about his feelings, I couldn't wait to see him in September. From the moment I awoke on the day he was returning, I moved around dreamily, slowed down by a cloud of excitement that made it difficult to breathe. I finally began to drive around aimlessly in the Camaro, since somehow I had to fill the hours until afternoon.

It describes me in a way I don't want to ponder to say

that at age eighteen, after living in Provo for a year, I had not explored it. I was a child without curiosity; I couldn't imagine caring about the neighborhoods beyond my own. So that morning, when I finally began winding through Provo one street at a time, I was struck by its lack of glamour. Unlike more trendy college towns, its downtown was characterized not by boutiques but by inelegant stores offering basic services—an optical shop, a shoe repair, a cubbyhole selling ammunition. As I cut across Center Street again and again into rows of old, dark, brick houses, I was startled that even in the unsparing light of Provo's sunniest season, the neighborhoods were dingy. The houses were very small—just one story and a full basement—and appeared unfinished and half sunken. Some of them also had whole conventions of weeds sprouting in the yards.

The entire scene bespoke neglect and a mild desperation that I couldn't fathom at first in this town that was about strong religious hearts finding their true courses. And then when a young Mormon woman surfaced out of the basement apartment of one of the houses, clutching her baby, I realized that this was a neighborhood of married students, whom I knew to be impoverished creatures.

Every day hordes of women like this one—wives—hiked onto campus with their babies on their hips. They streamed into the student center, plopped their children into booster chairs, and shared between-classes burgers with their husbands. They were part of the college landscape of young women with bright, lipsticked mouths and long eyelashes and pressed dresses. As I passed them on the sidewalks, where they often stood holding their husbands' hands before the men dashed back to classes, I believed that they led perfect lives. Yet this woman, the woman who was climbing out of

the stairwell that led to her apartment, was not thinking about
true love.

She was a couple of years older than I, with blond,
unstyled hair and a slight figure that had gone slack in the
middle with either an early pregnancy or the remnants of her
last one. She was wearing a pair of old-looking cotton pants
and a shapeless shirt in an artificial green that would have
looked characteristic only on a matron. Her remarkably pretty
face was not only pale with exhaustion but was as unadorned
as though it had just been whipped clean in the shower. While
I watched her, it never flickered with the slightest expression.

Her baby, whom she carried in her arms, was under a
year old and was tonelessly singing experimental sounds at a
near-deafening decibel level. The mother was numbly ignoring
the child. As though it took all her strength, she was completely absorbed in trying to get herself up the stairs with the
baby and the diaper bag. I idled along beside her as she hiked
up the street and then descended to the basement door of
another tiny house presided over by another young mother.
When the two women greeted each other, the blond mother
didn't smile.

Was this the paradise of married life, the exalted dream
of every Mormon girl? I had embraced the church's glorified
view of the sacrifices involved in marrying young and immediately starting a family—a view that makes the process an honor
and a prerequisite to a godly life. But it wasn't fulfillment and
godliness that I saw in the stilled face of that young woman;
I saw that marriage could be deadening.

It had never occurred to me, but almost as soon as it did
I felt delivered from the possibility. I knew that my efferves-
cence and optimism would save me—and also rescue Robert-
Peck—from the stern schoolmaster in his soul that might

otherwise rob our marriage of joy. I knew again, somehow, that there would be a marriage.

Back at my apartment, I waited for my Robert as though the months of deflation between us had not occurred. Excited and sure, literally hopping from one foot to the other with my impatience to close the deal, I realized everything I had to offer him.

I thought he had realized it, too. When he arrived, he reached out for me with his eyes and his arms, yanking me into an embrace so unqualified that all his soulless letters seemed like lies. His kiss was as exploring and sweet as a brand-new lover's.

Perhaps that kiss was the last battle in Robert-Peck's private war, where the godlike missionary battled the carefree boy. At any rate, when he stood away from me, his face held the kind of embarrassment and distaste you see on a cat when you hold it against its will. He seemed to be chiding me for the excitement he'd been feeling, managing at last to turn away from me completely and stand shoulder to shoulder with God.

I knew that somewhere in the middle, it had become a last kiss. The flickering faith in myself that I'd been able to feel sometimes even in the face of Robert-Peck's disapproval went out. I wouldn't feel it again for years. I had long accused him of knowing what I was worth, and there was nothing for me to do that day but once and for all accept the judgment.

Two

I

I am someone who had to get married, although not for the usual reasons, which is too bad. Perhaps if it had been for the usual reasons, I would look back upon the courtship with a little pleasure. Instead, I had to get married because someone insisted on marrying me in the name of God. To be fair to the man who insisted, I was very eager to get married before it was too late for me, although not necessarily to him.

I didn't find it absurd that I, a college sophomore, thought I was getting old, since the BYU world seemed to have decreed that a girl was ripe for only a few, sweet seasons. One of my roommates turned twenty-one that year, and as she puttered in the kitchen I stared at her gloomily and pondered becoming an old maid just like her. Marvella was a very pretty, unintellectual girl with a spectacular bottom that rode very high, but the number of young men who paraded after her through our apartment did nothing to shake my conviction that she was too old to land anyone. When she became engaged at the end of the year, I was shocked. I felt a rush of warmth for her and all humanity when she told me, the way you do when you read a news story about someone who has found love despite not having any legs. It seemed more likely that I would find someone, too.

My desperation was extreme, but not by much. Marriage is the backbone of Mormon society and doctrine—Mormons believe that only the married are allowed to enter the Celestial Kingdom of heaven—and the primary reason for BYU's existence. Ernest Wilkinson himself had urged us to pair off as soon as possible. "With approximately seventy-five hundred returned missionaries on our campus, this is by all odds the largest and happiest hunting ground in the world, and their success is attested to by the fact that approximately two thousand of our students marry each year," he told us during his emotional address at our freshman assembly.

The General Authorities who spoke at our devotionals also rarely completed an address without encouraging us to marry. (They have even periodically convened special, church-wide priesthood meetings via satellite TV, wherein they have scolded the church's young men that to remain single is to shirk their responsibilities before God.)

A message about speed was also being trumpeted throughout the mission field: Our campus was awash in stories about mission presidents who, upon sending their twenty-one-year-old missionaries back to college and normal lives, admonished them to be married within six months.

My own parents had told me they were footing the bill for BYU so that I would have the "opportunity to meet my own kind."

All this proselytizing was very effective: From the time I arrived at college, I was constantly assaulted by the sound of squealing. I'd spin around and there would be another coed standing on a sidewalk, flapping her suddenly bedazzling left hand in the face of a girlfriend who was ogling the ring while jumping up and down. In the winter, the girls were so bundled up in scarves and boots and coats that only their eyes and foreheads showed, and the one hand that the betrothed girl had freed of its glove. The snowy scenes were so alike and anonymous that they became symbols for marriage in my mind, the way drawings of the Madonna and Child signify motherhood for Catholics.

My own urgency to marry increased considerably after Robert-Peck rejected me on spiritual grounds: I desperately feared then that no worthy priesthood holder was going to want to marry me. I had so much to prove that I was willing to entertain the idea of marriage from even the most unlikely quarter. Which, as it happens, is where it came from.

One of the happiest circumstances in my life that fall was the fact that my brother Len had finished with his mission and come to Provo. I was very fond of my somber brother, but the real source of my delight in him at that time was his living situation. He'd installed himself in an apartment containing a remarkable number of roommates, and I had immediately begun spearing all of them with my eyes. In the aftermath of my broken romance I wasn't emotionally healthy enough to develop a preference, but one of them did. By Christmastime I was approached with serious intent by Monty Brown, who was the runt of the litter.

By this I partially mean that he was much shorter than I. I am five feet ten inches, though, and a lot of men have been shorter: Monty was remarkable because he was even less profound than I. His father was in international business, Monty had lived all over the world, and yet his observations about the human condition could have been written in his palm. His plans for the future were equally narrow: At age twenty-seven, he was planning to graduate in the spring and then pursue an advanced degree in accounting—not because he was interested in numbers, but because he wasn't more interested in anything else.

I cannot say that I was drawn to his neat appearance, which, though immaculate, was far from stylish. He was a stocky but very handsome man with a square face and remarkably strong jaw. He wore crisp, suave shirts and buttery leather slip-ons he'd bought during his mission to France, but much too often he combined them with an array of slacks that might not have wrinkled even if he'd wadded them up and forced them into his car's glove compartment. A great many of these trousers were plaid.

The incongruous nature of his wardrobe was matched up, with unfortunate exactness, to his hairdo. He possessed a great deal of black hair, and in the days before blow dryers, he somehow fluffed it magnificently into a lofty hat of hair that did not enhance his image, in part because Monty was such a peppy ballroom dancer. As we trotted around on the generous dance floors of BYU, his massive coiffeur rose and fell as though stirred by little gusts of wind.

The thing that made me take him more seriously as time went on was that he never saw himself as ridiculous. How he swaggered around—not sanctimoniously like Robert-Peck, but with a sheer unassailable sense of entitlement that was no less impressive to me because I couldn't fathom the reasons for it. I remember watching him return to me at a church social, across a tiled floor crowded with girls in pale dresses and young men in suit jackets. Surging through the crowd, he possessed a lot of physical grace and power for such a small man, and he appeared to half-strut, half-glide across the room. I was certain that his confidence promised a churning sexuality.

He immediately asked me to change my life for him, to quit my job at the student paper so that we'd have more time together. (As soon as we were engaged, I did quit, too.) He pressured me from the time we began dating to prepare his dinner every evening. (I never agreed, but the battles were fierce.) Although he made it clear very early that I was the woman for him, he was nonetheless quick to criticize my kisses, my clothes, my family. And he discussed the long line of his former girlfriends while his forehead puckered with displeasure at their failures, which he hoped I wouldn't repeat.

If Monty was often demanding, however, he also seemed barely able to live without me, and those flashes of vulnerability touched me. One night we were at his place, sprawled over a beanbag chair, and one by one the roommates trailed in from their own dates to cluster around us on the shabby couches and hear my tales of the day. Because of my position on the student paper, I always knew stories about personalities on campus or the conflicts over censorship that occurred between kid reporters and church authorities, and I told these stories in a lively way. The whole time I was recounting them that night, I felt Monty gripping my hand across the chair with a gently increasing pressure, as though he were trying to hold on to me. I glanced over at him and saw that he had closed his eyes, but that his face was still registering every word I said with rapidly shifting expressions of delight and doubt and pleasure. I had his complete attention.

When the others had gone off to their rooms, he reached over and touched my face with a naked fear of losing me in his eyes. "You are more fun than anybody," he said. "I am so proud of you."

I was still such a wreck over Robert-Peck that I was a pushover for a man who truly wanted me, and so my enslavement developed quickly. Within ten weeks of the time we began dating, I could feel safe only when Monty and I were together, when I had the shape of his emotions to mold my own against.

I didn't have long to enjoy these reassurances. Courtship wasn't therapy at BYU; it had an end. And although I wasn't planning to marry Monty, I began to love the idea that he would ask me. I began to hope that, in the BYU tradition, he would do so unforgettably, seeing as how some of my friends' fiancés had cooked up proposals that played like epic movies. One of my girlfriends had gone fishing on Utah Lake with a fellow who hired a scuba diver to plant the ring on her hook. Another's boyfriend dangled the ring from a tree branch along a BYU walkway where they often strolled together, and plucked it from above her head as nonchalantly as a hired magician pulls quarters from the ears of children at birthday parties. There were so many engagement high jinks going on that O. C. Tanner, one of the Salt Lake City's premiere jewelry stores, sponsored a monthly Great Engagements contest that rewarded the wildest efforts. I was hoping that Monty might think of something that would win.

When Monty did propose, the event had one major thing in common with every other milestone we would ever share: It did not resemble my dreams. The mood struck him while we were sitting in his battered car in the bare parking lot behind my apartment, staring at a back wall that was broken up only by small windows and patches where the paint was flaking. The only sound was the sputter and crunch of gravel beneath tires as other cars crept past us on their way into or out of the complex. It was a cold, dark night early in the spring, and Monty and I were hunched inside our thin jackets and irrevocably separated by a stick shift and bucket seats. Suddenly he turned to me and said commandingly, "I want you to marry me."

I froze. I kept trying to see his face clearly in the darkness, as though I would discover that I loved him if I could only make him out perfectly. Suddenly, unexpectedly, it seemed unthinkable to refuse him. Now that I was on the brink of it, my desire to be engaged was so great that it overwhelmed everything else. I had never been able to picture myself in bed with Monty, or working through a problem with him, or even talking to him for another year, but my need for validation had grown enormous.

I couldn't see that my plan to reel him in, then wriggle out of the engagement when it became too threatening, would hurt him. I couldn't see that it would hurt me.

I must have waited a full minute in complete silence. "Okay," I said finally.

Very soon we were standing up in my kitchen and kissing. I didn't like to stand up when I kissed Monty because this reminder of his lack of stature was humiliating. I was still at an age where my courtship with a short man seemed like a public statement of my inadequacy: Not only had I been unable to control my growth, but I hadn't managed to attract anyone my own size. I couldn't break out of such tunneled thinking, and yet I believed I could break the bonds of an engagement forged from 150 years of religious voodoo and every ambition my mother had ever held for me.

I was distracted from my discomfort at crouching when I felt Monty slide his hand onto my behind. It remained there confidently, cupping my buttocks, the fingers splayed so that I could feel separate pressure from each finger. The gesture was so outside the boundaries of our chaste courtship that I opened my eyes to study Monty's face. He was smirking a little.

He brought me the ring in a few days. He and Len rode into Salt Lake City as seriously as though on a military mission and returned with a one-third-carat diamond sitting up very high above a thin gold band. Monty and I drove out into an open field together, a patch of brilliant grass dotted with a few wildflowers, where he slipped the tiny thing onto my hand. For half an hour I stood beaming into his camera against a backdrop of the Rocky Mountains. One of the frames he snapped was of my freckled hand alone, with the ring glinting on it. When the pictures were developed, I sat with that one on my lap for a long time, staring in disbelief at the size of the stone. I couldn't fathom how anything so small could carry such weight. That ring couldn't have felt heavier on my finger if it had been a dictionary.

From the beginning, the ring symbolized only that I was pledged to marry someone I didn't entirely like; the pleasantries that I had imagined would be associated with it never materialized. I had thought I'd enjoy wagging it in front of my roommates and impressing upon my family members (and Robert-Peck) that I had succeeded at life. I had thought its existence would allow me, after I'd returned it to Monty, to be known as a girl who'd broken her engagement—a girl who'd been wanted. That reputation shimmered with so much honor and intrigue in my mind that I had thought I'd be able to slide through another couple of years searching for the real man of my dreams without appearing to be a spinster. Instead of these liberations, every time I glanced at the ring my stomach became a knob of nausea.

I began behaving as though the ring itself were the problem. I'd slip it off while washing my hands and watch it twinkle from its precarious perch on the basins of BYU's public bathrooms. I'd leave it on the nightstand while I slept, or secure it in my locker during my modern-dance classes. I always felt much better when I wasn't wearing it. Finally I began to see that I couldn't wait, that I was going to have to break up with Monty right away.

I never considered simply pressing the ring into his palm and saying, with infinitely more honesty than had characterized our relationship thus far, "I don't love you." I had never in my life performed an act that direct or filled with self-esteem. Part of the problem was that I wasn't a very brave girl, but I also didn't feel that what I wanted or didn't want was a good enough excuse for not marrying a righteous man who desired me, particularly in the man's eyes.

I needed a reason that was incontrovertible, even to a priesthood holder. And one night, lying in my big, blank room in the dark, washed over with the wheezy rhythm of my roommate Hannie's breath as she slept, I remembered it.

II

In those days, most young Mormons were searching obsessively for The One. Today, church authorities try to discourage youthful romantics from believing God has selected a marriage partner for them before birth, and that He will make that person known if He is properly asked. But it has been an uphill battle for reform: The concept of The One lends itself too perfectly to the Mormon passion for spiritualism. I know a thirty-six-year-old single woman who, just last year, tore over to her sweetheart's place in the middle of the night and stormed around and around his bed, weeping inconsolably. It seems that he wouldn't accept her revelation from God that he should marry her because he was The One.

The belief in The One might seem to the outside world to be at odds with the practice of polygamy for which Mormons are still most famous, but polygamy was never practiced by the majority of church members and was largely irrelevant to young Mormons by the turn of the century. At BYU we all expected to live out our lives in conventional marriages, and I know of no one who has done otherwise. Although polygamy is still practiced today among fundamentalist Mormons who are pointedly excommunicated when discovered by the mainstream church, although some of my childhood friends in Arizona were descended from polygamous grandparents, my peers and I thought the practice did not relate to us. (I never even heard the word *polygamy* until I was eleven years old, when I came running in from school to tell my mother, with more amazement than pain, that someone in the schoolyard had taunted me with the fact of my father's many wives. She explained polygamy to me as a historical event, something that had gradually ended when declared illegal by the U.S. government in 1862 and banned later by the church itself. She said that polygamy had no place in our lives. Through the years I became aware that my father didn't completely agree— he rarely missed an opportunity to declare that men are "polygamous by nature"—but since my mother paid little attention to these posturings, neither did I.)

I certainly believed personally in The One—my love for Robert-Peck had been unshakable in part because I thought he had The One written all over him. Since our breakup I had been distracted from my search for The One by the dishonest intent and chaos of my engagement, but I remembered it now, and remembered that I had never believed Monty was The One.

Which is what I told him. He had let himself into the apartment one night and I could see that his brown eyes were filled with feeling for me. Sometimes the pigment in Monty's eyes seemed to be opaque and lying near the surface, but that night their depths were limitless, a tunnel that bored through to his heart. I should have realized that he really loved me, or believed he did. That he wasn't going to relinquish me easily.

"I'm having a lot of doubts," I said to him from across the room, before I could lose my nerve. "I mean, we haven't even asked Heavenly Father about each other. We don't know that either of us is The One."

Impatience flitted across Monty's mouth and eyes. "Do *you* want to marry me?" he asked.

"Yes," I lied. "But I'm not sure it's the right thing. I think we ought to pray about it."

"All right, we'll pray about it," he said comfortably. He sat down on the old sofa and held out his arms. I walked into them reluctantly, thinking it was one of the last times I would have to.

I truly thought that Monty would pray sincerely, searching for a revelation, and that God would tell him to leave me alone. I certainly couldn't admit the truth to myself—that I had accepted Monty's proposal without any intention of following through and was now using God to get me out of it. That I expected fate or God to solve everything.

Or perhaps I believed that nothing painful could come from Monty's prayers. When I was nineteen, I felt that every excellent moment of my life was the result of prayer, my constant companion. I spoke to God as inevitably and casually as though He were a girlfriend, often chattering aloud to Him when I was in the car or alone in the apartment. I prayed because I needed someone to confide in and also because I thought I might receive advice: The principle of direct, personal revelation received through prayer is the bedrock of Mormon theology.

Although I hadn't gotten any specific instructions from heaven yet, I had gotten comfort. And I did know the language of the revelations that were occurring on all sides: Most of the people I knew at BYU who received revelations, including marriage revelations, claimed that "God had told them it was right." The people who said this were usually men, and the two facts had become connected in my mind. So I sent Monty off to pray and didn't pray myself, partly because I assumed without praying that we weren't meant to be together, and also because I didn't feel very powerful. I believed that because I was a woman I shouldn't take any initiative. I also believed I shouldn't *have* to take any.

If I'd been thinking clearly, I'd have realized it was a dangerous move. I knew other men who'd become very aggressive after consulting with God about the future, and I knew that all around me coeds were bending to heaven's will in matters of love.

Wayne, for instance, a roommate of Monty's, had received a marriage revelation about Mary, a young woman of his acquaintance whom he wasn't dating when the revelation arrived. On the surface, these two were very alike. They were intelligent and small; they were uninterested in clothes and obsessed with the prospect of travel, to the point that much of their spare time was spend in the school library poring over issues of *National Geographic*. They appeared to have so much in common that even without a revelation, a marriage between them would have made sense to a lot of people.

It didn't make any sense to Mary, though. When Wayne told her of God's will she was preparing to leave on a mission, an activity that attracted a great many of the church's faithful young men but only its very most devout young women. Wayne pleaded with her night after night until he took on an exhausted, haunted appearance; his face became pale and his hair began falling into his eyes. Then one night Mary phoned he'd gone to bed nearly defeated.

, she'd finally prayed over the mat-

same thing: The two of them were

ayne came bounding out of his room

his coat on through a dazed delight

ered him blind and unable to punch

eves.

ce after that. She was on the sofa at

lding Wayne's hand, wearing a long

printed with flowers. There was some-

er eyes.

n?" I asked her.

king it on faith," she said. Monty later

len in love with Wayne right after the

where they wanted them.

Well-rested with a playoff-opening night off, the Badgers were set to welcome Chaparral up north, just 24 hours after the Firebirds had topped Goodyear Millennium for the right to advance to Bill Shepard Field at PHS where Prescott hadn't lost a game in two months.

But in the end, the higher-seeded Lady Badgers, who entered the 1999-00 season as the state's No. 1-ranked 4A girls' soccer team, could only sit and wonder what went wrong in Chaparral's 2-1 win to end their season one game short of a State Tournament Quarterfinals berth.

At the beginning of the year, now a distant memory back in early December, the Lady Badgers

I also knew about the revelation granted to Jacob, an original thinker who, despite Mormonism's inflexible emphasis on marriage, had always felt that love for one woman might somehow dilute the love he could offer mankind. He'd been sharing his plan never to marry with a friend during the moment when it was revealed to him that, despite his misgivings, he was meant to marry Elizabeth, someone whom he'd known for years. He received such an indelibly spiritual message that the memory of it carried him through a courtship that in twentieth-century America was ridiculous.

For although Elizabeth accepted Jacob's carefully worded offer, he felt no differently about her than before. She did not compel him. In fact, he kissed her only once before their wedding, and he even saw her rarely, since he was studying for his orals.

The engagement was purgatory for Elizabeth, who loved Jacob and is a woman whose strong, graceful body seems to fill a lot of space because it gives off so much sexual power. She was seeking an ardent match. She probably wouldn't have married Jacob at all if she hadn't received her own revelation one night while she was doing the dishes. She told me that she clung to that, though, and she and Jacob have four beautiful daughters now. They are crazy about each other.

These stories about coercion and conversion were the ones I knew about marriage revelations, and yet I was startled when Monty finally described his own.

"What sort of revelation?" I wanted to know, when he told me it had been received at last.

"Well, it wasn't a burning bush or anything," he said a little sharply. "It was just a good, warm feeling that said it was the right thing for us to get married."

The information paralyzed me. I thought he was telling me the truth, of course. It didn't occur to me that a righteous priesthood holder would use the sacred tradition of revelation toward his own ends.

My brain began scrambling for God's reasoning, for juncture points between Monty and me that made us intrinsically right for each other. I could not find anything. Neither of us possessed passionate interests or plans for the future, and I thought that together we were likely to wander through time as impotently as a couple of trapped flies.

I also felt horribly confused by Monty's assertion that his revelation was a *feeling.* How was a person supposed to tell the difference between a feeling that was a revelation and one that was just a . . . feeling?

I pulled out of the circle of Monty's arm a little and told him I wanted to try for my own revelation.

I remember the prayers that followed not only because they were agonized but because they were so atypical of the way I prayed. I scooted into my apartment in the middle of the day, when it was empty. I dropped to my knees and threw my arms over my bed in a gesture of desperate supplication. Day after day, I half lay there railing at God over the unhappy prospect of living with Monty. At least I started out railing; soon I would float into a mindless torpor that made my engagement seem completely unreal. By then I had lost touch with the fact that I hadn't been serious about Monty in the beginning. I was really trying to know the right thing to do.

"I'm not feeling anything," I said to my fiancé. "Not *anything,* except that I seem to be floating in space whenever I talk to God about you. It's the most terrible feeling."

"I know what that is," Monty said. His voice was very taut. "That's just Satan trying to interfere with what the Lord wants us to do. *Satan* is doing that to you."

I was more lost after that because Satan was so real to me—was a major player in the cast of spirits that had paraded through my thoughts and dreams since childhood. More than once I had heard my father cinch his point in an argument about money with my mother by telling her that her spend-thrift attitude was Satan's work going on inside her. He had often told me that the women's movement was Satan's way of trying to weaken the family. Actually, Satan and his literal servants, whom we called "evil spirits," took the rap at home for everything my father considered ungodly, and they still do. In recent years, when my mother realized that her maid was making off with the silver, my father (who was fond of the maid) announced with complete conviction that the theft was the work of an "evil spirit." His belief in the influence of the spiritual underworld among mortals is absolute.

So I simply didn't know how to ignore Monty's pronouncement. I truly began to fear that my feelings toward Monty were the work of the devil.

I was brushing my teeth one night when these fears reached a peak. I was imagining what it would be like to marry Monty, to lie down with him naked and feel his skin next to mine. This seemed like a safe alley for my mind to wander into, because I liked the idea of finally discovering the sex act. But it wasn't safe that night: My knees turned to soft knobs of putty and my stomach fell into them. I sat down abruptly on the toilet, and the hem of my long nightgown trailed into the puddles of water I'd left standing on the floor after my bath. When I tried to rise again, the clammy hem got tangled up between my legs. The mere effort of trying to disentangle it as I rushed to the phone brought me close to tears.

I was calling Monty, but my brother answered. "You and Monty have got to come over here and give me a blessing," I said. "Satan is trying to keep me from marrying Monty again."

They arrived very quickly. Len's shirttail was hanging out, and he was too impeccable for that; I realized that they had dressed in a screaming hurry. They found me perched on my bed with my knees drawn up under my chin. When I tried to speak, my teeth chattered. I was making such an effort to keep from screaming that my voice came out thin and sharp, as though I were angry. I believed I was possessed.

My dreaded sweetheart and my brother stood on either side of me, pouring a few drops of olive oil onto my head out of a tiny bottle—"consecrated" oil that had been blessed for this purpose and that priesthood holders keep on hand in the medicine cabinet. They laid their hands on my head and with the power of all Mormondom behind them rebuked the devil, commanding him to leave me.

I had asked Monty to deliver the incantation, and Len told me later that he resented it; it is a privilege that he thought should be kept within the family. Certainly the only men who had ever blessed me before, on the occasions when I had been ill or very troubled and had needed a powerful priesthood advocate with God, had been my father or brothers.

I understood the significance of my selection, though. When I assigned the holy task to Monty, I surrendered to him as my husband for the first time.

III

I have told the story of my engagement to Monty often during the many years since I have recovered from it. I've told it to friends unfamiliar with Mormon ways, and to psychiatrists who can barely control the amazement that wants to spread across their faces. All of these people have asked me the same thing: "Why didn't you tell your parents what was happening and let them help you?"

Certainly my parents would have wanted to help me, but I seemed to have quit knowing my parents. Across the thousands of miles between us, I could not recall that my daily happiness mattered to them. What I did remember was that they had expounded since my birth upon the importance of my marrying a certain kind of man, and that Monty was the kind. I thought that the many years of my parents' advice about what constitutes a suitable marriage—not just their spoken advice, but the more powerful variety that was made out of their own and their parents' lives—was pointing toward Monty as my exact destiny.

In the beginning, my parents taught me about marriage through stories about my grandmother, Thelma Baker. So far as my father has been able to determine, Thelma was the first Mormon ever to live in central Florida, where she moved as a teenager at the turn of the century. She was a fierce and beautiful woman whose belief sustained her through the many years it took for the Mormon missionaries to begin proselytizing in Florida and provide her with religious fellowship. Even that long isolation wasn't her major test of faith, however: That would have been the fact that it took her seventeen years to convert her husband, Leonard Laake, to Mormonism, and then another nineteen to save the money that allowed them to travel to Utah and go through the temple together. Only then was her civil marriage "sealed" in the unique Mormon ceremony that makes it binding after death.

My parents spoke admiringly of Thelma's conviction that God would soften Leonard in time, but they also wagged their heads often over the chance she'd taken. What if Leonard had never come around and she had been left husbandless in the next life? So I had known from childhood that I needed to find a fellow who was willing and worthy to take me to the temple right away—a lifelong member of the church who was as steeped in the notions of eternal Mormon marriage as I was. There weren't many young men who were lifelong Mormons in the small ward in Florida where I grew up, and so this qualification of Monty's that was only an accident of birth impressed me beyond all proportion as our engagement progressed. It made me believe on a level I couldn't reach that my parents would think Monty was just right for me.

I also became tangled up in the rule I thought my parents had lived by: that a temple marriage is so paramount as a prerequisite for happiness in heaven that a longing for romance on earth should not be allowed to interfere with it.

They have been married for fifty years, but I have never understood what caused my mother and father to choose each other. As a young girl, my mother, Bobbie, was vividly ebony-haired and high-spirited, whereas my father was beige all over and, because he was so sober and self-belittling, had seemed to be fifty from the time he was born. Mother has always said she loved him in the beginning because she loved his friends—the few unassuming Mormons in Tampa who welcomed her and converted her out of the ranks of the less fun-loving Methodists into a life of lively parties. She was twenty when she married and not profound, and she enjoyed kissing my father. That and a sociable community seemed reason enough to wed.

She left my father when I was ten. Our family had migrated to Arizona by then, and Bobbie and I journeyed back to Tampa for the summer, where we stayed with her sister in a marvelous small house with a deep lawn. For the first time in my life I was allowed to share my mother's room, and throughout those exiled months of tropical heat I watched from close range while her face trembled with the strain of her life coming apart.

When the summer ended, she folded her clothes into her suitcase with as much difficulty as though she were bending wire. After we returned to Phoenix, I would sometimes hear her crying through the door of her room at night when my father was away on business, and her constant unhappiness filled the house like foul gas. Sometimes she sat on the edge of my bed in the evenings, smoothing my hair and trying to reassure me. "Your father and I have been married in the temple," she would say to me, with something like a smile. "That means our marriage doesn't end with death, and that you children will be part of our family in the next life." She explained that my school friends couldn't know this about their futures, since, as non-Mormons, their parents had gotten married in another kind of church where they spoke the words, "Till death do us part."

"Those children will be all alone after they die," she told me. "It's awfully important, Debbie, that your father and I stay together." She said it as though I were the one needing to be convinced.

And so it was that in the days after Monty tried to cast Satan out of me, I never looked to my parents as allies. Instead, I looked to Monty as my spiritual protector and tried to love him.

He was very strong and dear while I whimpered. He swept in the door after classes and pulled me into his confident arms; he held my head against his shoulder until my doubts seemed to calm down. For a while, he even prayed with me at night, as though we were already married and he was conducting family prayer. With great tenderness, he pulled me down onto my knees beside the sofa and kept an arm gripped around my shoulder while he pleaded with God for my peace of mind. My roommates saw his devotion and said admiringly what a fine priesthood holder he was, and after that I couldn't wait to get to him, to cling to him, when he came through the door. Once in a while, I thought the relieved feeling I had in those moments was love. I may have believed it as much as I believed anything.

It was that feeling that enabled me to whiz through the rest of our engagement without succumbing to despair. Soon we had created a huge, gay, snowballing ritual of congratulations that sometimes shouted down my fears.

IV

Monty and I were lying stretched out on the bed in his room, kissing and butting our pubic bones through our clothes. It was a Sunday afternoon and the apartment was finally quiet because all the roommates had left for church. We often stole a few minutes together after they had gone, minutes when we could relax and know that no one would interrupt us. We never spoke of it, never said, "Good, we're alone," but Monty's breathing deepened and sometimes his hands began to creep toward my breasts as soon as we had heard the door slam for the last time. I felt myself become boneless in his arms. Then, always before our passion could go any farther, we leaped up and raced out the front door ourselves. We slipped into the back pew in the chapel, our faces still flushed, as the opening hymn was ending.

But this particular Sunday was different. I was suddenly distracted by an intense burning in my groin—or at least "burning" is the word my brain located for the sensation that hit me with the forward momentum of a bullet train. I gripped Monty with a determination so single-minded that he was reduced to a lump of thigh. And after seconds of friction, my groin finally erupted with such sharp, sweet pain that I was holding my breath and gulping in air at practically the same time.

It didn't take long. It didn't last long. A moment later I was filled with a sinner's sorrow.

I pulled away from Monty, who had begun to buck and writhe. I can only imagine what it was like for him to be so close to a young girl's first orgasm and unable to follow his instincts.

"Something has happened," I said. I was holding him off me with some difficulty. "I don't know what it was."

He finally flopped onto his back and stared at the ceiling. "What did it feel like?"

"It felt wonderful. I can't describe it."

"Do you think it could have been a climax?" He posed this possibility with enormous gravity and a little excitement.

"I don't think so," I said. I had no idea what to expect from a climax except that I expected a much bigger deal. Something overpowering and shared, that justified the way couples who experienced them together in the movies kept locking eyes for the rest of their lives. Certainly more than just pleasure that had sealed me within myself, a million miles from Monty. "I don't know what it was. But I think we're getting too involved physically. I don't think we should be necking like this."

I sat straight up in the bed. "I think we should pray for forgiveness," I said. "I think we probably were petting."

All I knew about petting I had gleaned from a BYU health-education class and a professor with petting on his mind. One day he had very carefully drawn a diagram of a buxom young woman on the blackboard, and then he had circled first her head and throat and labeled it "necking" out to the side. Next came a ring around her torso, labeled "light petting." Finally he emphasized the most forbidden zone of all—below the waist—and labeled it "heavy petting."

I felt very grateful to this man, since my Sunday-school and youth-night teachers had been warning me against necking and petting since before such activities seemed attractive, but had never defined the parameters of sin. I was relieved to see that I had not yet seriously transgressed them, and Brother Jensen's artwork welded immediately to my conscience.

Yet here I was, straddling the stubby leg of a suitor whose face I didn't even want to see as my climax ripped through me. I slid to my knees, by the side of the bed. "Come on, you lead the prayer," I said to Monty. I felt fully confident about badgering him, since Mormonism doesn't engage in double standards when it comes to sex. If we had crossed over the line, I thought that Monty might be even more to blame than I, since the priesthood holder is in charge of every situation that matters.

He finally joined me on the floor, but he didn't show up as a natural religious leader that day. As he was beseeching the Lord to forgive us, I got the feeling that he didn't really mean what he was saying.

And in any case, prayer couldn't erase the memory of my climax, neither the thrill nor the confusion. We were both so interested (and in the dark) that we finally approached my gynecologist with our question. We sat in front of the doctor's big desk and held hands across the space between our chairs while I described the new feelings in my loins. I tried to be very exact, as though I were describing the symptoms of a disease. I wanted to be still an innocent girl, wanted the doctor to tell me that what I'd experienced was as unincriminating as a fever.

The gynecologist was a very prominent Mormon man in Provo who may have been accustomed to amazing questions from young girls getting ready to marry. "You are having climaxes," he said matter-of-factly. "You don't have to remove your clothes or have sexual intercourse in order to climax."

He turned to Monty then, in a spirit of hearty congratulations. "You are a very lucky man!" he said. "You're getting a wife who's very easily aroused!"

Apparently the doctor didn't think I was lucky, since he didn't say anything to me. And as I trailed out of the doctor's office with Monty's arm slung around me, I felt unlucky in a thousand ways. I thought it was unlucky that a climax had nothing to do with being uncontrollably drawn to someone. It was unlucky that it could be experienced mechanically simply because another, not entirely unattractive, body was near my own. Primarily, though, I felt unlucky to have gotten so soiled without even knowing about it. I wasn't able to distinguish between having an orgasm at the conclusion of the sex act and having one without it. I mean, if petting was a sin, I thought that orgasms must be off the scale. And I'd had one without being married. And hadn't known to stop. And might not have stopped if I'd known.

And didn't stop. That was the thing that disappointed me in myself the most. Once I knew what I was doing, I kept right on. If anything, I squirmed against Monty's thigh more than I otherwise might have, hoping that orgasm would forge a connection between us. But it never did.

It was in this uneasy frame of mind that I visited my bishop a couple of weeks before the wedding, to discover whether I was worthy to be married in the temple.

Not just anyone can go to the temple; you have to qualify. If either Monty or I failed during our separate interviews to give the proper answers to our bishops' strings of probing questions, we'd be reduced to a wedding held in a mere Mormon chapel, the garden variety building where Sunday services take place and where marriages are binding only until death. I had never personally known anyone to whom such a disgrace had occurred, and I didn't want to be the first disgraced person whom my friends knew, either. And yet a primary criterion for worthiness among would-be templegoers is sexual purity—something I was no longer sure I could lay claim to. Monty wasn't troubled by this concern; he would later breeze through his interview with his bishop, a different bishop from mine, with so little trauma that he didn't even share the details. But I was terribly nervous as I drove across the campus to meet with Bishop Hensley.

I hardly knew the man; we hadn't exchanged twenty words that year. He was small, with thinning hair and a friendly manner that also communicated he didn't have much time. Almost without preliminaries he launched into his litany of questions while I sat before him in a patch of sun streaming through the window, feeling spotlighted.

The first queries were easy and expected. Do you attend your meetings? he asked me. Pay a full tithing? Support your church leaders? Do you avoid tobacco, alcohol, coffee, and tea?

I had always done all these things—had known I would have to do them if I were ever to be granted a temple recommend, the magical document that would allow me to pass by the sentries and enter the temple on the day of my wedding.

"Are you morally clean?" he asked finally.

There was only one way to interpret the question. It had nothing to do with honesty or ethics or the other activities of intention that the world refers to when it uses the word *moral.*

In the church, the word *moral* is assigned exclusively to the realm of sex. This is such a given that no one even remarks upon it.

I had meant to feel Bishop Hensley out about his own interpretation of "moral" sin, since it can vary: What is sin to one bishop is understandable to another. But this turned out to be another moment like the one when Monty had popped the question and my prior intentions to refuse him had fled. I found myself just vigorously nodding at Bishop Hensley.

I learned about his interpretations then. "Well, all right, so you haven't slept together," he said very cheerfully. "But what about this other stuff that's sinful—this necking and petting stuff? How far has all of that gone? I know that things can get out of hand during engagements."

I like to think I had planned to confess if it came to this, but I'm not sure I ever did plan to. I don't think I was equal even in my dreams to allowing the truth to cut me off from my ordained future.

And since I was going to lie anyway, I really went for it. "We haven't done anything like that," I heard myself saying too loudly. "We've been very, very careful. We've known exactly what was wrong, and have avoided it."

To my astonishment and relief and dismay, Bishop Hensley didn't suspect a thing. (Wasn't he supposed to be inspired by God?) He signed the form quickly with a smile that wasn't quite directed at me and I fled into the hall.

I ran all the way out to my car. It was the deepest part of spring in Utah, when the air is thick with bees and scent, and the power of the day assaulted me as I ran through it. The contrast between its beauty and my own seemed very great. For several minutes I slumped against the car door, unable to accept what I had done. I thought no one had ever done it before.

Three

I

On a morning in early June, Monty and I climbed into my parents' long car and sailed off to Mesa, Arizona. I wore a red dress, short-waisted, of a fabric so rubbery you could have used it for waterproofing, and Monty's slacks were green plaid. We huddled close together in the backseat, swathed in unintentional Christmas colors, while my diminutive father steered through Scottsdale's streets and my mother clutched in her arms the foamy billows of my wedding gown. We were headed for the temple.

For as long as I could remember, the Mesa Temple had been the focus of my most unbridled imaginings, a presence so grand it could not be dwarfed by twenty acres of lush lawn. My parents had traveled all the way from Florida to be married in this temple. Then when I was small our family had lived in Phoenix, which adjoins Mesa, and I'd ridden past the temple on Mesa's main street and had walked in its gardens a thousand times. It was the only site I'd considered for my own wedding.

But until my wedding day, the interior of the temple itself had been forbidden to me. I understood nothing of its exquisite sacraments. Although the most significant rituals of Mormonism go on within its temples, and although the Book of Mormon itself warns against secrecies in religion, the temple ceremonies are nonetheless top secret outside temple walls, lest their sacred strangeness be ridiculed and defiled by nonbelievers.

Now the morning when it would become clear had finally arrived. *My* morning. Many of Mormondom's young men visit the temple for the first time when they are nineteen, on the occasion when they become full-time missionaries, but most women enter the temple initially as brides. There they participate in a wedding ceremony unlike any other in the Western world and—this is what I believed—come to understand at last a host of planetary mysteries.

The universe will open today, I was thinking as Monty and I undertook that protracted drive. I wouldn't have been surprised if God himself had shown up at my wedding; my faith felt that buoyant. And Monty's mood easily matched mine. He was jammed up against me in the backseat with a jaunty eagerness I would not experience again until it was with another bridegroom.

It's a quirk of the Mormon wedding ceremony that Monty and I weren't actually going to be married that day; instead, I was going to receive my "endowments." (Monty had received his own years before, when he'd left for his mission.) These are sacred ordinances and promises that make a person eligible for the highest heaven, and Mormons partake of them on their own behalf during their first visit to the temple. In the years to come, I would be expected to run through the same ceremony again and again as a proxy for dead ancestors whose names had been discovered through the Mormon pastime of genealogy. (The idea behind the temple is that certain ceremonies, such as baptism and marriage and the "endowments," are vital to a person's placement in the hereafter and yet can be performed only on earth. Unless conscientious mortals turn their attention to the graceless states of those who've gone on, scads of wishful spirits will flap around in limbo for eternity.) Taking out my "endowments," in addition to being a very serious business, was a prerequisite to the marriage ceremony, and is tiring enough that many Mormon brides elect to postpone their wedding ceremony until the next day.

We pulled up beside the temple's velvety grounds, and my mother spilled out of the car first, hoisting my gown in its crackling plastic bag. As I tucked my hand inside Monty's elbow and we mounted the stairs to the entrance, I could already see the Arizona heat shimmering off the temple's concrete walls in waves. We pulled open the large doors and found ourselves in a big lobby. I recall it as long and narrow, windowless as a tomb and yet oddly light. Everything in it appeared to be upholstered: The carpets were thick, the chairs padded, the population of largely middle-aged church members was plump. At one end of the lobby was a long wooden counter manned by temple workers, as though you might check your coat there. Templegoers were renting items of the all-white ceremonial clothing they would need during the temple rites ahead; the clerks were sliding across the counter dozens of white slacks and shirts and dresses that zipped up the front and looked limp from too many washings. I was glad that my own temple clothes, starchy with newness, were beside me in the imitation leather valise that was one of many wedding presents from my mother.

A couple of my parents' friends were awaiting our family; they were leaning forward off the edges of chairs pushed against the far wall, their feet out in front of them in shoes that were a little orthopedic. My two oldest brothers and their wives were there, too, still in street clothes. I was awfully glad to see them, particularly my eldest brother, Ernest, whom I'd always been close to, and whom I wanted near me during the moments when I would discover new meanings of life during the temple session.

Among the well-wishers was Laverne Reese, one of my mother's oldest friends. She was a second mother to me and the real mother of David, my comrade through summers of backyard adventures in childhood and, now that we were older, the object of some of my unspoken romantic fantasies. Had he not been the son of a permanent family friend, David would have seemed to me everything I'd ever wanted in a man, not just in terms of his religious history but because he was taller than I was. As things were, I'd never been able to admit my crush to him and risk a rejection I'd have to confront forever because of our families' intimacy. To the world, and to some degree to myself, I'd transformed my longing for David into friendship and had been hoping he'd go through the temple with me that morning. I asked after him.

"He didn't think he could stand it," Laverne said a little grimly, and I stood looking down at her for a minute suspended in time, stunned by the intimation that David might be jealous of my impending marriage to Monty. I found myself filling with longing for marriage to someone chosen not by God but because of my own feelings. I was still immobilized with yearning when Mother whisked me away, up the wide and elegant staircase.

Our first step in the temple journey took place in the brides' room. Mother had explained to me that it was the most luxurious dressing area in the temple and was reserved for women about to become wives. (After tomorrow, whenever

I visited the temple I would don my ceremonial clothing in a
locker room.) The wide chamber was rose-colored and shad-
owed and very sweetly swank; its deep upholstered chairs and
benches were pulled up to ornate mirrors where I could sit and
examine my uncertain face. My mother, who was still lugging
my voluminous gown around, hung it up with some relief,
then came with me into a private cubicle where she helped me
out of my clothes and into a "shield" the temple provided.
This beautiless thing seemed to be a white cotton sheet with
a hole cut in the middle for my head. It was open at the sides,
and I was naked beneath it. As I exited my cubicle five other
brides were exiting theirs in their shields. We looked like girls
in headless ghost costumes.

I padded along to be "washed and anointed." My heart
pounding, I climbed onto a stool in a small area made private
with curtains. Around me, coming from within other booths,
I heard hypnotic murmurs from the voices of old women. I
could picture the women exactly. Throughout my life, I'd
watched the faces of Mormon women settle into untroubled,
crumpling moons that began to look alike by the time the
women were old enough, and idle enough, to be "called" by
church leaders to positions as temple workers. (Older men
were "called," too.) Temple "callings" were an honor: They
were reserved for the most righteous of Mormons. My mental
image of the temple had become one of hushed rooms and
hallways peopled by a thousand perfect grandmothers. Their
faces and figures were round from pastries; their eyes were
bright but not deep; their frames of white hair were carefully
crimped. The creases that had come into their cheeks appeared
to be not only the slackness of age, but the deepening of their
complacency.

In a moment, my temple worker glided in, and her face was the one I expected. It was also very kind. "This is your special day, dear," she said.

Her gentle hands darted beneath my sheet to bless the parts of my body. There must have been a basin in our cubicle, because when she touched me her fingers were wet. She intoned, "I wash you that you may be clean from the blood and sins of your generation." She touched my head ("that your brain may work clearly"), my ears ("that they may hear the word of the Lord"), my mouth and lips, my arms, my breast and "vitals," my loins ("that you may be fruitful in propagating of a goodly seed"), my legs and feet. Her chanting and her cool fingers were both song and dance, and I was caught up, calmed. When she had finished the first round she began again, replacing the water with oil from a dropper that anointed me head to toe. I was tingling with significance now, the magic of unknown things. Finally the temple worker leaned to my ear to whisper my "new name": Sarah.

With that, the trance of body worship was broken. I didn't know what this new name was for and the conditions attached to it disturbed me. I must reveal it to no one, not ever, except at the one proper moment during today's ceremony, the temple worker told me.

Her demands made my stomach a tight coil of nerves. I hadn't mentioned it to anyone, but my major misgiving about taking out my "endowments" was the secrecy. I'd been known to be careless with secrets, especially when they were a colorful variety. I admired Monty and all the others who had been quiet about the temple ceremony all these years, but I doubted whether I would carry on the tradition with exactness. What would they do to me?

I was coming up now on the only part of this morning

that I'd been truly dreading: It was time to climb into my first pair of regulation Mormon underwear, an unlovely wardrobe item that, during their first temple visit, Mormons agree to wear for the rest of their lives and that they refer to ever after as their "garments," as though their underwear is always the only clothing they are wearing. In those days garments were one-piece, made of thick nylon, and cut like very loose teddies; they had a scoop neck and little cap sleeves and they came to the knee. The amount of coverage wasn't accidental: One of the purposes of "garments" is to make sure that Mormons eschew daring clothing. The other is more directly theological: The underwear's holy nature is expressed by small markings sewn into the cloth over each breast, the navel, and one knee. (The markings signify comforting homilies like "Deal squarely with your fellow men," and are intended to serve as reminders of temple covenants. The symbols themselves derive from the fact that Joseph Smith was a newly initiated and enthusiastic Freemason when he originated the Mormon temple rites in 1842, and so the Masonic compass and square appear on the left and right breasts of the Mormon garments.) The garments had one other characteristic that, if not actually biblical, did have something to do with creation: Women's garments were slit in the crotch, very generously, so that they flapped open and left a girl's greatest fascinations exposed.

They were unwieldy indeed, and yet the garments I've described were the streamlined, modern, everyday variety. The pair I received on my wedding day were specifically designed to wear inside the temple itself and were patterned after the garments worn by the original Mormons in the mid-nineteenth century.

I was wearing long johns.

The fabric was thick and white, probably a cotton blend,

and it reached to the wrists and ankles. The neckline was so high that I realized it was going to poke above the square cut of my gown.

Swathed again in my shield, I trailed dejectedly back to the bride's room. I was met there by a replica of the washing-and-anointing woman, who gathered me and the other brides into a little flock and admonished us kindly that we should wear our garments "night and day." She said to wear them next to the skin, with our bras over them, and explained that they represented the garment God gave to Eve in the Garden of Eden. Unless we sullied them, our "garments" would be a shield and protection against the power of Satan until we finished our work on earth.

I knew to take her seriously. One of the major themes of mystical Mormon lore had to do with those who have sailed unscathed through death-defying circumstances on account of their garments. The most oft-repeated stories involved un-named wartime soldiers who'd watched bullets glance off their clothing as though it were armor, and vaguely identified fire victims whose burns halted wherever the boundaries of their garments began. I had never questioned these particulars. On the contrary, I had treasured them, especially when they described someone I knew. I still remembered affectionately the occasion when my friend David's father had survived electrocution and I had heard my mother tell my father, "He never would have lived if he hadn't been wearing his gar-ments." At least at that moment, the clumsy clothing had seemed to be more than a mean-spirited conspiracy against sex appeal.

On the morning when I was first blanketed in garments, they did not. My brain whirred with visions of movie-star fashions that I'd never be able to buy, the way they say you see your whole life pass before you as you drown. I felt I was leaving behind me forever the worlds of desirability and youth. Standing resentfully before the beaming temple worker, I figured I was going to hate my underwear every bit as much as I knew my mother hated hers each day that she put it on. Mother had never said as much to me; she had always referred to the donning of her baggy underwear as a privilege. But she was a fashion plate, and many was the time I saw her patting futilely at the ridges this amazingly extensive covering made across the rump of her sleek clothes. I had watched her flip through a hundred racks of dresses at Goldwater's, pausing with a beat of longing at the sleeveless dresses that the cut of her garments outlawed. These griefs of the soul didn't even begin to take into account the misery of wearing nylon armor during the summer.

I figured that from this moment on I was a freak.

As I prepared for the temple session, a long look in the mirror did nothing to reassure me. Decked out in my wedding finery now, I appeared to have dressed at random out of a weird laundry hamper.

It wasn't just that my underwear had become a feature of my wedding ensemble, seeing as how it encircled my throat for a fully visible five inches. It was also that, instead of my delicate mantilla veil, I'd had the temple veil foisted on me. It was a swath of fairly sheer, limp fabric, gathered around the head as though by elastic and otherwise unadorned, which my dress was not. It lay across my hair as heavy as though it were wet. I couldn't seem to stop staring at myself.

Of course, Mother noticed my interest. She was not as concerned as I about my ensemble, because sartorial glitches did not pose an aesthetic problem for templegoing Mormons. A lot of women brought only street-length white dresses to these sessions, and their special temple garments jutted out beneath the hems so that the women looked like Sikhs. But Mom was eager to be sensitive to my mood. "This isn't anything to worry about," she said levelly, rustling away and returning with a dickey for my throat that the temple matrons kept on hand for just such occasions. It wasn't the same shade as my eggshell dress, and its lace bore no relationship to my gown's tulle, but I was going to have to live with it.

"You look like a beautiful *Mormon* bride," my mother said, and I hoped Monty would agree with that.

II

As soon as our little brides' room party was ready for the temple ceremony, we all flowed out into the main crowd of worshipers. Glancing around at the other brides, I felt my heart lift as I realized I looked no more eclectic than anyone else. Monty was ahead of me in the throng, surrounded now by all three of my brothers, who were jostling and teasing the groom in a relaxed way that I attributed to the fact that they'd all been to the temple before. At one point, my ordinarily unsmiling brother Len threw his head back and laughed unrestrainedly.

Like everyone else entering the temple service, these four wore white shoes, socks, pants, shirts, and ties. I thought they looked like angels. Across their arms they'd draped articles of ceremonial clothing to wrap around themselves during the upcoming ritual's appropriate moments. The most eccentric of these regulation accessories—a green satin apron sewn into the shape of a fig leaf—was dangling very low off Monty's arm like a long streamer off the body of a philodendron. That bright leaf bobbing among sets of legs was the last I saw of Monty for a few minutes as he merged with the mob of shimmering templegoers.

We filed quietly into the cavernous Creation Room, where huge and staid murals depicting the creation of the earth loomed above the pews. The paintings were brilliantly colored, and against these frescoes of horizons and meadows and peacefully grazing beasts the chapel full of white-suited worshipers shifted and stirred like a field of daisies. The men took their places on the right side of the chapel, the women on the left. I was seated next to a particularly radiant bride. Her joy was so overpowering that its light nearly triumphed over the sad-sack effects of her temple veil.

The temple ceremony is on videotape now, but at the Mesa Temple in 1972 it was all still done live. Temple workers played God, Jehovah (whom the Mormons believe was born into the world as Jesus), and the archangel Michael (who became Adam), three separate beings who seemed to be in the process of creating the earth together. This first part of the service was a dramatization of the belief in the plurality of gods.

The temple workers were not good actors, and the unreality wasn't aided by the fact that there were no sets or costumes: The performers stood before us woodenly, in front of a curtain, in the simplest of temple clothes. They appeared to be merely reading their lines. Even after the story turned to the tale of Adam and Eve and the serpent, my attention wandered. When instructed to do so, I tied on almost unconsciously my own green apron, a symbol of the fig leaves that had first clothed Adam and Eve. (The ceremonial use of aprons is another similarity between the Mormon and Masonic rituals.)

I came to life only in the moment when Elohim asked Eve and the women in the congregation to promise to obey their husbands in all things so long as their husbands obeyed God. I had known that some heavy pledges would be required of me today, and this one—known as the Law of Obedience— was the first. I made the promise easily. Next came the Law of Sacrifice, where we convenanted to give up all we possessed, "our lives if necessary," in defense of the church.

Now we were getting somewhere.

I kept catching Monty's profile across the room beneath his unlikely hat. I couldn't imagine how I hadn't noticed the hat before. It was made of cloth and was bouffant; it resembled a chef's hat that has been subdued. It attached to his shoulder with a ribbon and a snap, lest it fall and be defiled by the floor. I stared and stared, hating the way he looked in it. I was still brooding about it when I noticed something going on around me that captured my undivided attention.

Elohim had just instructed his onlookers to learn to perform a grip, a special handshake, that he called "The First Token of the Aaronic Priesthood." (There were to be several of these handshakes, and they, too, were strikingly similar to ritualistic Masonic gestures.) Everyone had practiced the handshake with a neighbor. And now Elohim was asking us to make a sign, as though we were slitting our throats "from ear to ear," to signify the penalty for revealing this handshake to anyone on the outside.

All around me, as nonchalant as though they were yawning, a hundred smiling Mormons in white were drawing their thumbs across their jugulars. It's a testimonial to the thoroughness of my Mormon upbringing that I reacted to this first bizarre moment with only mild surprise.

The God of my Mormon ancestors had always been represented to me as whimsical, in some way human because of his former life as a man. Within this context, eccentric acts on His part were understandable. I had, after all, come to believe at last that He might have chosen me and Monty for each other. I did not expect Him to constantly make sense.

How else, except in terms of eccentricity, could you explain the fact that His interests lent themselves to introducing polygamy into America? How did you explain his capricious standards for behavior, as demonstrated by one of the great object lessons in the Book of Mormon, the murder of Laban? Laban's murder was a slaying that God himself commanded one of his favorite mortals, Nephi, to commit for a cause! The killing had been touted to me from Sunday-school class right through BYU religion courses as an example of how anything is right if the commandment comes from the Lord. The thing my teachers read to me about Laban was the expansive reasoning of Joseph Smith, who had said, "That which is wrong under one circumstance may be, and often is, right under another. God said, 'Thou shalt not kill'; at another time He said, 'Thou shalt utterly destroy.' "

On the day I went to the temple for the first time, the world had not yet experienced the rash of famous Mormons, from bomber Mark Hofmann to impeached governor Evan Mecham, whose consciences may have been aided during dark acts by this doctrine they'd heard since birth. The phenomenon of a conditioned people that believes what it is told, and that sometimes justifies actions beyond the limits of decency set by most of the rest of the world, was still hidden away within temples where I was being asked as a matter of course to protect a secret handshake with my life. Was hidden, too, within the nature of my indoctrinated heart, which believed it should make the promise.

The jarring moment passed, and we all followed along to the next chapel, which was called the Lone and Dreary World room. It was painted with flat faces of desert scenes, with brown vistas stretching endlessly and with prehistoric carnivores battling in the foregrounds. The light in these paintings was stark, so that the hostile animals didn't even cast shadows. We were to believe these were the sorts of surroundings Adam and Eve had called home once they'd left the Garden.

Here the play continued. Satan paid a preacher thousands of dollars to teach Adam about God, and the preacher described a God who embodied the concepts embraced by many Protestants. "Do you believe in a God who is without body, parts or passions; who sits on top of a topless throne; whose center is everywhere and whose circumference is nowhere; who fills the universe, yet is so small He can dwell within your heart?"

These ideas were ridiculous, and so Adam shooed the corrupt minister away. Then Elohim sent the ancient prophets Peter, James, and John onto the scene to banish Satan. Satan departed, but he wasn't a good sport about it: Before he vanished, he had the last say.

"I have a word to say concerning this people!" he cried. "If they do not walk up to every covenant they make at these altars this day, they will be in my power!"

His threat overtook me with a chill. I was truly terrified. Immediately, I began reviewing the covenants I was making, fearful I would forget one and damn myself.

Now the old-time prophets turned to the congregation and explained, "You are now ready to be instructed in all things pertaining to eternal life." It was the cue for temple workers to turn their attention to teaching us more "tokens" and "penalties"—the ritual hand motions and pledges to punish that underscored every temple service, and that were sometimes identical to the "tokens" and "penalties" found in Masonic ceremonies.

We learned the Sign of the Nail. The name seemed to allude to the Crucifixion, and the gesture was a matter of pressing index fingers into each other's palms.

We learned the Sure Sign of the Nail, a handclasp wherein we linked little fingers and pressed our other fingers against our neighbor's pulse. I practiced both of these exercises easily with the happy bride beside me, wondering a little why I needed to know them.

The "penalties" to be extracted for revealing the new maneuvers were by now much harder to get through. My stomach flipflopped as, in unison with my brethren, I acted out cutting out my heart, then a strong slash low on the abdomen to disembowel myself. I didn't understand whether I was promising to submit to death at the hands of someone wielding the switchblade of justice or whether I would be expected to take my own life if I found myself blurting temple secrets, but as time passed I performed these brutal pantomimes with increasing reluctance. Once I even felt bile flood my throat, and I wondered why I was overreacting. No one else was responding to the drone of threats as though it were sinister. In fact, as the macabre instructions from the stage grew more graphic, the smiles surrounding me seemed to widen.

I glanced behind me and found my mother in the next row. She was fiddling with her ensemble, trying to adjust the extra articles of clothing that by now we were all wearing. In addition to the aprons, we were swathed in "robes" of white pleated material that wrapped around our trunks diagonally, as though they were very bulky beauty pageant sashes. Over my flowing wedding gown, these additions made me look as padded as a little kid trussed into a ski parka. My mother was looking puffy, too, and she was trying to bring herself into better alignment, but when I caught her eye her face leaped into a smile so filled with love for me and confidence in these rituals that I was able to believe there was something flawed in the way I was perceiving the action going on up front. I looked over for Monty, too, wanting him because he would steady me if he could. But instead of finding him, I intercepted a glance of pure hunger and heat being dispatched by the husband-to-be of the lovesick girl next to me. As their eyes met, their need was a laser beam in the room. My envy ached in my joints.

I was relieved to be distracted at last by the parting of the curtains. Behind the stage, the drapes disappeared and revealed what seemed to be a very long bedsheet suspended from the ceiling. It had deep slits cut into it that were about the same height as an average man—slits that matched the markings of the temple garments except that they were much longer and larger.

I saw Monty then because he was also looking for me and grinning as though something important was coming— perhaps something that would make these rococo temple rites make sense. As I moved with the others toward the bedsheet, we were told that it symbolized the veil that separates this life from the next. A handful of male temple workers had taken their place on the other side of it and thrust their arms through the slits, and one by one the audience members were reaching their own arms through to embrace the workers they couldn't see, who in their positions in the "afterlife" represented God. When my turn came, the routine altered a little: The person who took his place on the other side of the veil was Monty. It was he who would usher me into heaven. It always happened this way for brides, who unlike the men had made their temple covenants not to God but to their own husbands.

This embrace through the veil was by far the most intimate thing Monty and I had ever done together; our furtive groping sessions could not compare with it. In fact, the idea of sharing the secrets that join the dimensions with a man to whom I'd never been able to tell the deepest secrets of my heart made me shy as I approached the veil. Coaxed into it by another one of those kindly female temple workers, who had appeared to stand beside me, I slipped my arms beneath Monty's and then around him. I moved in close so that through the sheet our bodies were touching as though we were dancing.

The temple worker now asked that we touch at the "five points of fellowship": foot to foot, knee to knee, breast to breast, hand to back, and mouth to ear.

And then, when Monty made the Sign of the Nail into my hand and asked me to identify this "token" and its "penalty," I realized disbelievingly that this was a test. The actions that were going to guarantee my entrance at the gates would have nothing to do with love or charity or the other teachings of Christ that I'd been raised to believe God valued. In fact, I hadn't heard a single one of those words spoken today, the most primary day of religious instruction in my entire life.

No, I was going to burst into heaven on the basis of mumbo jumbo. God must never have gotten past that carefree period of mortal development when he'd formed a club with little pals and refused to let them into the tree fort without a password. The mysteries of the world were fraternity rituals. A wild, bewildered giggle was forming in my throat.

What in the world was everyone doing? Did all the white-suited glorifiers in the room unquestioningly accept a ritual of nutty gestures from the pseudo-occult as a sacrament?

Those were the first moments when I viewed Mormonism with suspicion, and yet my turn at the veil was nothing like a full-blown awakening. The tiny flames of anger licked through me and then went out, just another of the brief savage caprices of my wedding day. I quickly began concentrating, trying to believe my fiancé's muffled incantations were scriptural truth.

I reviewed with him all the "tokens" and "penalties" I'd just learned, and I came to know at last the purpose of my "new name" when Monty asked me to reveal it to him. "Sarah," I said directly into his ear. It was the secret, magic password that would identify me to Monty at death so that he could pull me through to the other side. Without Monty, I learned in that moment, I wasn't going to get into heaven at all. That's how the system worked for women, although I would never know Monty's "new name." Apparently God himself ushered in the men.

Now Monty was whispering into my ear the final token of the ceremony. "Health in the navel, marrow in the bones, strength in the loins and in the sinews," he intoned. "Power in the priesthood be upon me and upon my posterity for generations of time and throughout all eternity." Then he commended me for passing the test: "Well done, thou good and faithful servant, enter you into the joy of the Lord."

We joined hands in one of the secret grips, and he pulled me through the slits in the veil.

We were in the Celestial Room, named after the uppermost tier of complex Mormon heaven, and the most notoriously decorative room of the temple. Vast and hushed, crowded with fussy furnishings and lit with chandeliers, it was populated with dozens of bent heads above fig-leaf aprons. Most of the prayerful were seated in deep chairs along the walls but a few were kneeling, away from the foot traffic emanating from the veil. I could have gladly dropped to my knees myself, but the quest for peace of mind was postponed as my family and Monty's family, all of whom had apparently passed through the veil ahead of me, crowded around to sweep me into a series of congratulatory embraces. The temple ceremony was completed, and Monty and I were well on our way to becoming man and wife.

Later, dressed for the world again, my first pair of daily "garments" already sticky with sweat beneath my suffocating street dress, I tried to tell Monty a little of what I was feeling as in that awful ovenish weather we walked across lawns that seemed to go on for miles between the temple and the car. "It wasn't what I thought it would be," I said. "I expected to hear things that would make me feel inside the way I feel when I'm singing the hymns I love the best. You know, when it all comes together in your heart and you know that what you're involved in is the right thing?"

"And you didn't?" he asked, without much understanding. His arm came around me and pulled me against him, the ledge of my shoulder hitting inches above his. His face was changed by his passion for the things we had just gone through together. "Boy, when I brought you through the veil, that was something."

III

On the final day of my wedding, when I would actually become Monty's wife, the first thing on my mind as I awoke was my eccentric sleeping arrangement.

I was entangled in a situation born of my desire to get married in the Arizona temple. Since my family didn't live in Arizona, my parents had rented a two-bedroom furnished apartment in Scottsdale that summer and, upon our arrival from Utah a couple of nights before, had installed me and my betrothed in the room with two single beds. "I guess I can trust that nothing will go on in here?" my father had asked sternly, looking hard at first me and then Monty.

He spoke as though Monty and I found each other wildly compelling, a not unreasonable assumption. I reassured my father with cheery confidence, however. Even then I realized that I was drawn not to Monty but to orgasms, an activity I wasn't likely to pursue in close proximity to my parents. I knew I wouldn't encounter in that room a temptation I couldn't resist unless somebody interesting came in through the window.

In keeping with the theme of avoidance that had characterized my engagement, though, I didn't consider until that last morning the ramifications that pallid attraction would hold for my marriage. I waited until I was watching Monty's stocky outline lying beneath a sheet six feet from mine to admit that, although he didn't repulse me, whatever lay between us was too thin to occupy us for long, in bed or otherwise. Even this close to the embargo lifting, I felt no urge to slip in naked beside him as a surprise.

And even if I had I wanted to, I wouldn't have known exactly what to do next. My parents had harkened so well to the church's promotion of innocence that the entirety of my direct knowledge of sex, if you didn't count the health-class drawings and my rather chaste orgasms, had been obtained through a series on sexual disease that had run in the local paper when I was a teenager and an odd presentation that had been presided over a couple of weeks earlier by my gynecologist. Unfortunately, the doctor's attempt at sex education hadn't sunk in very deeply, on account of my embarrassment.

It wasn't that the information itself had embarrassed me; it was the setting. This particular Provo doctor must have been in great demand for the premarital services that BYU kids required, since he had hit upon the idea of group orientation as a way to increase efficiency. On a second visit that Monty and I undertook so that more things could be explained to us, when I had expected to have the pleasures of marriage described to me privately, we had found ourselves instead herded into a meeting room where perhaps fifteen couples sat on rickety folding chairs exchanging equally rickety smiles and nervously holding hands.

"Is anybody here not a Mormon?" the Mormon doctor had asked loudly from the front of the room. "I give a slightly different lecture in that case."

But no, we were all Mormons. In fact, I knew quite a few of the kids in the room because they attended my ward. I did not know them well enough, however, to desire to share with them the slide show of brightly colored genitalia that followed. "Since you're Mormon kids, you probably don't have any experience," the doctor had said matter-of-factly while the projector beeped and various views of vulva and testicles loomed on the wall. "I recommend that as soon as you're married, the first thing you do is turn each other upside down to see what you've got. Get acquainted."

I'd found myself wondering suddenly about the upside-down appearance of a red-headed fellow to my left whom I'd always thought seemed interesting when he spoke in church. And then I'd flushed a color I didn't know was lurking within me as I realized that others in the room might be wondering about my upside-down appearance. About the only concrete thing I took away from that lecture was a pamphlet about positions that showed human beings to be as lithe and sexless as elves.

The enormity of my lack of preparation and passion might have overwhelmed me on that last morning, except that, as I used the curling iron and put on another coat of nail polish, I allowed myself to pretend that I was going to find the last-minute grit to career off to Mexico alone in my Dad's big car. I told myself that Monty would recover from his disappointment and that maybe even God would. Perhaps there was even some way to sort out the problem that only Monty knew my "new name"; maybe I could encourage my mother to yell like hell for Sarah when she got to the other side.

I was still considering escape, my throat filled with misery as thick as phlegm, when my brother Ernest whooshed in the door bearing the wedding gown that we'd dropped the day before at the cleaner's. "It's a good thing you know what you're doing, since all the important stuff happened yesterday," he teased me from across the room.

And I thought, Ernest's right; I'm as good as married already. I went along to the wedding very meekly.

We were joined forever in one of the temple's small, unadorned "sealing rooms," kneeling on opposite sides of an upholstered altar. We clasped hands across the altar's silky top while the temple president, Brother Sorenson, bathed us in spontaneous marriage advice of which I haven't the slightest memory. Inside Monty's hands, my hands felt hot. At one point I gazed out at our audience—a sparse one of our family members and a few friends, all of them Mormons worthy to enter the temple and all of them dressed in white. My father caught my eyes and nodded to me, his own eyes inscrutable. The room's bright lights reflected off his bald pate and turned it as white as his shirt. I thought he was blessing me. For the first time, and for just a moment, my wedding was possessed of the serene dignity I'd always imagined.

Just then Brother Sorenson invoked us to gaze into the hallway toward a wall of mirrors whose unending reflections symbolized the eternal nature of temple marriage. He was an old man, and as he pointed at the mirrors with his thin hand he completely forgot what he was saying; his voice weakened and then died. Monty and I and our well-wishers stirred uneasily, but then Brother Sorenson resumed with new energy, and Monty and I were married.

Usually the mother of the bride cries at weddings, but in this case it was the bride. Our party adjourned to the Celestial Room, where I began weeping onto the collar of Monty's shirt. I couldn't seem to stop. His hands on my shoulders felt firm and sure, and for a wild moment I considered telling him what I was feeling, since I imagined he might be strong enough to help me. The thought disappeared behind a couple of hiccups. "She's just thinking about what she's done with her life," my new father-in-law joshed.

Maybe Monty was thinking about the future too, apprehensively, since he immediately began pointing out ways that I was failing him. We hadn't even left the temple grounds before he was growling that I was willing to surrender too much time to family shutterbugs who were intent on pictures. And when he and I stopped at a coffee shop for lunch after the ceremony, our first hour alone in days, the occasion was consumed with his horror that I planned on tucking into not only a man-sized meat-loaf sandwich but also the potato salad. He ranted and raved that I should save my appetite for the reception, which, in the Mormon tradition, wasn't scheduled to begin for six or seven hours.

I absorbed all this with wholly shocked surprise. Lest I notice a million things I couldn't have lived with, I had loped through our engagement with my eyes fastened unswervingly on racks of wedding dresses and catalogs of invitations. Now here I was with a man who was revealing a mentality for the smallest concerns imaginable.

In spite of everything, I enjoyed our pretty reception, which is still immortalized in the album of photos showing Monty changed into a tuxedo with the pants legs too short and me in the unstylish gown I thought was perfect. We are standing near the country-club entrance with linked arms, and we're gazing at the photographer as though we can't wait to be alone together and are just humoring his need for artistic expression. In other pictures, our smiles are so wide that our teeth reflect light. Once I'd calmed down, I enjoyed my bride's role that day, the same way I'd enjoyed my role of bride-to-be. The approval and attention of onlookers made me feel I'd succeeded at something important.

IV

As I'd whirled around on a Scottsdale patio in Monty's arms, in my father's, in my brothers', I'd wondered if I would ever again be so completely the center of attention. But of course I was, almost immediately. As soon as the door closed behind Monty and me at Del Webb's Townehouse, a hotel in downtown Phoenix, I was the only thing on Monty's mind. I was so unnerved by the intensity of his eyes upon me, by the way he homed in close and buried his face in my neck, that I fled into the bathroom to change into my blue, beribboned nightgown. I felt blessedly alone in there.

It was only ten o'clock when we climbed into bed, but it had been a very complicated day. I was tired and terrified, and relieved when Monty suggested that we wait until later. It wouldn't have occurred to me to suggest it, since I thought that the moment of consummation was his decision.

Each of us was wearing our garments and our nightclothes over them, so that between us we possessed nearly enough raiment to populate the Paris season. Thus insulated, we lay marooned together in the center of the king-sized bed. I was afraid to touch anything. I was afraid he wanted me to touch something. We fell asleep immediately.

The deed itself was accomplished before it was light, and was a fumble I'm glad I had to live through only once. I can't imagine anything more graceless than the coupling of two virgins. I was particularly horrified by Monty's upside-down appearance. It was *nothing* like those slides.

We were both so confused that we quit trying to finish

at some point. We lay together holding hands as sunlight came into the room. I couldn't look at Monty.

We decided to go downstairs for eggs; we were kids, really, and we thought that room service was too grand for us. In the last minutes before we were preparing to leave the room, I was swabbing on mascara in the bathroom and congratulating myself on the maturity I'd shown by not mentioning to Monty my disappointment in his lack of sexual knowledge. Although Mormonism demands that both young men and women be virgins when they marry, nobody ever said a guy couldn't ask his married buddies for a few pointers. I was wishing he had, and I was also deciding that I would.

Standing in the doorway to the bathroom, Monty stood watching my ablutions with a face that had suddenly become drawn and closed. I didn't understand his expression, unless it meant that his disappointment was even deeper than mine. I didn't understand what he said, either, which was, with every word ice-cold and underlined, "I didn't know that sex would be something *you* were going to have to learn how to do."

The years have allowed me to adopt an attitude of affectionate wonder toward the kind of self-delusion that would enable a completely inexperienced twenty-seven-year-old man of no particular allure to blame sexual failure entirely on his partner. But at the time I felt like he'd heaved an ax between my eyebrows. His cruelty shattered the frail intimacy that had sprung up between us in bed a little earlier, and in its place was all the clawing panic I hadn't allowed myself to unleash that morning. The weight of a million damning facts about Monty and me filled my stomach, my chest, my throat; it snaked down my legs and made my feet throb. When Monty, having delivered his salvo, retreated to the bedroom, I shut the bathroom door and leaned against it, heaving not with sobs but with desperation. Trying to pull myself together, I slid down into the crouch of a baseball catcher and bounced nervously, wrestling honestly for the first time with the thought that the God who from my earliest memories had wrapped Himself around my heart, who had always been kind to me, couldn't want this—and that, even if He did, if He were really that arbitrary, maybe marriage to Monty was something I just couldn't do for Him.

I managed to bide my time for a few minutes until I heard Monty leave the room for something, but then I streaked to the phone like someone trying to get around a kidnapper. I had never been happier to hear my mother's voice. My announcement was so staggering to her that she tells the story still as a family legend, how the morning after she'd been contentedly unwrapping my wedding presents my shrill voice was tearing into her sweet memories of marrying me off. How I was talking about something that families rarely welcome, and particularly Mormon families.

I choked out to my mother, "This is terrible. I don't love this man. You've got to help me get a divorce."

Four

I

I think that if we hadn't gotten married in the temple for what we both believed was eternity, Monty and I would have recognized right away that we'd made a youthful mistake best remedied by a swift annulment; I think that very shortly my parents and I could have reduced the whole thing to a rueful family joke. Instead, my parents worried themselves to death from the moment of my frantic phone call, but because of the serious vows I'd taken, they couldn't really counsel me to immediately throw in the towel. Instead, Monty and I recovered from the wedding night as best we could and plunged into the future, as though spending the rest of our lives together was something we'd be able to make ourselves do.

I was very lonely that summer and fall, for experiences I didn't even know enough to want. So often I awakened beside my small, warm husband and wondered what I could be feeling if I had awakened beside someone else. Then after a while I quit wondering, because I'd become so insulated from everything, even my own desires. So little was stirring between Monty and me that for a while it was as though I'd been put to sleep by the fact that we never really touched. Although, even if we had known how to or had wanted to, touching would have been difficult. We were separated as irrevocably as though we were always in different rooms by the ever-presence of our garments.

We always wore our garments when we were lounging around the house. I always wore my street clothes as well, since I felt unappealing in my garments alone. Monty and I never were able to run our hands lazily along the hollows of each other's bare bodies while talking or reading; we never knew the pleasure of running into a wall of willing flesh while turning over in sleep. I still can't even form a mental picture of him that doesn't include thick layers of nylon.

The only time we didn't wear our garments was during sex, but they greatly influenced our sex life anyway. When I'd received my garments in the temple and been told by my temple worker to "wear them night and day," the instruction had seemed impossible. I'd turned to my mother for specific instructions on when garments could be removed, knowing that she would enlighten me in the way that Mormon parents had been passing down the details about garments according to their own biases since Joseph Smith had designed the first pair. My mother revealed herself to be not fanatical but not exactly a liberal thinker either. It never occurred to her that I should bathe in the things, for instance; I've heard of a few zealots who've stepped out of their garments with one leg, washed and dried the leg, and then stepped into a clean pair. No, she told me to remove my garments for showers and sports and sex but to wriggle right back into them once I'd finished. "Then you will feel very clean and sweet before your Heavenly Father," she said.

I followed her instructions with an exactness she may not have meant, bobbing up worriedly the moment Monty stopped writhing. I insisted that he do the same, nagging him in a voice like Alice Cramden's. Perhaps my Heavenly Father was satisfied with me, but I don't think Monty ever was.

Our conjugal relationship was also plagued by condoms that had achieved extraordinary stature, and that were the last few inches of numbing membrane that relentlessly separated us from each other and sexual adventure. Like the interference of garments in our sex lives, the grave routines that accompanied our condom use could also be blamed with at least some accuracy upon a parent, in this case my father, who had taken it upon himself to make sure that for us condoms would never be a simple matter of squishy packets tucked away discreetly in a drawer.

The night before we were married, my father had propelled Monty onto the patio of the Scottsdale apartment and presented him with a package of lambskin Trojans and a lecture. He had done this at my request, since I was both ignorant about birth control and impressed that my father had managed to limit the number of his own progeny to four. In the outside world four was a courageous number, but it was on the low side of respectability in our culture, where clamoring mandates from church leaders discouraged birth control and encouraged enormous families that would cause membership rosters to swell. I had asked Dad to share with Monty not only his successful methods but whatever stout attitudes of the heart had enabled him to take a stand against the advice of the authorities he usually devoutly admired. Like my mother before me, I didn't want to spend the rest of my life pregnant, and I was grateful to my father—a political archconservative and a man with the stern demeanor of an Old Testament prophet—for his occasional liberal lapses that made my life easier.

Dad had really warmed to his assignment, perhaps out of concern for me but certainly because he is the most creative saver who has ever lived, a paragon of financial caution so extreme and original that he is as great a genius in his way as was Leonardo. He has purchased excellent houses and cars and educations for our family members, but this largess never thinned his resolve to remain a chiseler on the small things. I have never known him to be not absorbed in sweet imaginings of untried ways to cut trivial expenses to the bone. And no incident has better illustrated his remarkable talent for finding them than the instructions that accompanied his gift to Monty, wherein he explained that the condoms in question were expensive ones—costing more than a dollar apiece—and should be reused.

He didn't leave it there: He included elaborately detailed instructions for laundering condoms, instructions that I believe he had never tested. I can't imagine that my fastidious mother ever permitted the recycling of condoms, and she certainly wouldn't have allowed them to lurk around the house while drying out, rinsed free of sticky substances and stretched out long and flat between layers of tissue. No, I think my father had been silently watching his investment in pricey condoms vanish for thirty years; I think he passed along to Monty a wistful plan for penury in the way that parents often hope to see their children fulfill their own most cherished dreams.

I think this *now*. At the time I thought he was all-knowing. And so Monty and I set out to manifest my father's personal vision the way we did everything, as though we saw no alternative to the wisdom of our betters.

Condoms were always taking a rest around our place. After use, we lathered our hands and scrubbed the condoms inside out. Then we left them on top of the toilet tank, shrouded in tissue. Or we secreted them inside cupboards, which we then cracked open a little so the rubbers wouldn't mold. Whenever we actually needed one we had the choice of several, all of them by then as unbendable as fire irons. Monty would throw one into a basin of water to soak, and after it was pliable he would run tap water into it to check for leaks. He rarely found any; the condoms were of amazing quality. I would recommend them to anyone. The original package of twelve lasted us the entire year. That was one of the outcomes.

The other was that my only experience with sex was of shockingly cold, ill-fitting and clammy sheaths that once in place transformed Monty's penis into something inhuman. Sometimes I would watch my husband approach the bed while flapping the moisture off a condom that was fresh from the bathroom sink, and I would think it was lengthening like stretched taffy, until it was the most monstrous thing in the house.

II

All marriages have emblematic stories, or at least all of mine have. With Monty there were three, and they brought us full circle.

The first incident, the one that foretold everything between us, occurred during our honeymoon in Colorado. All through our protracted drive through the Rockies, up into dramatic mountains and through canyons that to this day I have never seen, I withdrew from my new husband by reading with a degree of absorption that almost completely discouraged interruptions. I started with stacks of *Redbook*, which in 1972 was littered with references to the Women's Movement, then in full swing, references that kept me stirred up with outrage at the antics and ideals of Women's Libbers. "I think Women's Lib is destroying the country," I said to Monty disgustedly once, in what probably constituted my sole comment to him before nightfall. "Women don't know how to be loyal to their families anymore."

Later on I turned to *The Group,* Mary McCarthy's study of the sexual adventures of upper-class eastern girls and by far the most provocative novel of my life until then. I don't recall why I had brought *The Group* along, but I know that once I had stumbled upon the blossoming, erotic psychologies of Lakey and Helen, I disappeared as completely as though I were riding in the trunk. "What are you reading that's so interesting?" Monty asked me at one point.

"This is a book about girls who aren't particularly nice," I said.

"Well, I don't know if you should be reading that. What's it like?" He asked it with that sense of silly excitement you hear in the voices of people who are new to sex, and I didn't even bother to answer him.

And that was pretty much what our honeymoon had been like up until the morning we went for breakfast in Ft. Collins, a morning when I believe Monty was determined to regain my attention.

We settled on a coffee shop with panoramic windows and a reputation for biscuits. "I want the steak and eggs," I told Monty almost immediately, although not without some trepidation. I had become slightly apprehensive about my hearty eating habits since his wedding-day haranguing about the potato salad and a few subsequent comments that had likened my appetite to that of a normal male athlete. I was realizing that food—*my* food—was going to be one of our issues, and this feeling was quickly confirmed.

"It's the most expensive breakfast here," Monty complained.

That, of course, was the heart of his concern with consumption. Monty was a tightwad who would finally disappear out of my life still whining that I owed him seventy-five dollars. During the first tender days of our marriage he'd griped again and again about the price (forty-seven dollars) of the corsages for our mothers, practically the only wedding expense that had befallen him, and he had propelled us from one motel to the next in the evenings, searching during the hours that were supposed to be some of the most sensuous in our lives for a rate that was a dollar or two cheaper. I had borne this penury uncomplainingly, primarily because I wasn't talking much.

But during the moment when he quibbled over my desire for a big breakfast, I reached a saturation point. The truth was that we were far from pressed for cash. Motivated by a tax break, my well-off father had just given us as a gift easily enough money to see us through Monty's years in graduate school. I was feeling far from comfortable with my discovery that Monty, like my father, was a born chiseler on the unimportant things.

"I know it's more, but I'm hungry," I said to him about my breakfast selection, my voice steely.

His face became thoughtful and the muscles within it gnarled a little, as though with concern. "I don't really mind that you have the steak and eggs," he said finally. "But when you want something expensive like that, there's a way I want you to ask for it. Say, 'I know it's the most expensive thing on the menu, but can't I have it, please, honey?' " He laughed a little, but his chuckle was a hard sound; it seemed to me a message that he knew he was being ridiculous but didn't intend to back down. Then he repeated the last two words of his little speech, drawing them out until they were the wail of a child. *"Pleeeezze, hooonnney."*

With life-altering clarity, I thought I heard his pleasure in his new husbandly power, his conviction that it was his right to control me, saturating his voice. I thought he was peering at me expectantly, as though he knew I would immediately begin to burble his very words.

I behaved so reflexively that I surprised us both. I reached for the car keys and slid out of the brown booth and strode the length of the restaurant while he watched me with a concentration that was as yet unperturbed. I think he couldn't imagine that I would really walk out on him. Even as I burst through the glass doors I could see him still at the table, his hands just beginning to come unfolded. I was very calm as I unlocked the car door and slid behind the wheel. When I actually started the car Monty came rocketing out of the restaurant, and the impression of his great animation just grazed the sides of my eyes as I drove past him.

But as I wound around the block a dozen times, at first so furious that I couldn't perceive anything beyond the bright green hood of the car, I began to feel a little chastened. I mean, what had Monty done that was beyond my understanding? Hadn't I often heard my own father, the priesthood holder, try to order my mother around? And hadn't the source of much of their unhappiness together been her refusal to allow it? Hadn't I meant to support Monty in his holy "calling" as the head of the house, and not repeat my mother's divisive mistakes? Wasn't Monty the representative of God in my life?

In my heart of hearts, I could not have believed all the upright answers I was giving myself to these questions. But as

I had with my doubts about marrying Monty, I dismissed any messages from my heart of hearts as the murmurs of the devil. By the time I turned back into the coffee-shop parking lot, I had willed myself into meekness. I was determined to scale to the heights of Mormon womanhood—to become a model helpmeet—with willpower alone.

When I pulled up in front of Monty, who was still pacing on the sidewalk in front of the restaurant, I clambered elaborately over the console to take my place again in the passenger seat. I listened quietly to the rise and fall of my husband's indignation that may have gone on for half an hour. I did not find an excuse for avoiding lovemaking that night.

The second incident occurred when we visited Monty's parents in Akron that same summer. One joyful afternoon, a rare few hours when we felt playful and at peace with one another, we decided that we would shower together. We stripped off our clothes in his mother's studied white bathroom, tossing them against the bleached counter tiles. The clutter and color were as jarring as though our shirts and slacks were huge stains.

Once in the shower, I found myself staring at my husband curiously, as though I'd never seen him naked before. I noticed how undefined his large muscles were, that despite his otherwise bulky stature, the bones in his feet were aristocratically fine and the hair that covered his feet and legs was wispy. Even his gestures were small and almost fragile as he slid lather over his broad chest. On previous undressed occasions, during lovemaking, I hadn't perceived that there was nothing truly powerful about him.

It was quite a revelation. I had always been bothered that Monty was short, but now I knew there was not one heroic element to his stature. I knew that the man I expected to usher me into heaven was nothing more than a mortal, completely destructible.

I minded his humanness for a moment, but in the next moment I was freed. When I saw that Monty was just an average man without muscle tone, I realized that although he was the priesthood holder, he might not always be sure of the best way to run a marriage and might not be able to teach me. It struck me that perhaps I had expected too much from him and too little from myself. And that perhaps I had never before expected anything of myself beyond compliance.

Embarrassed by all I'd ascribed to him, I reached over to kiss him as I finished bathing, a kiss of compassion. As much as I was ever able to savor anything between us, I savored that kiss. Then I reached to slide the shower door open.

"Wait a minute, I haven't finished," he said.

"You don't have to hurry." I smiled at him. "I'll leave you a dry towel."

"If you get out now, you'll get my mother's carpet wet." I realized that he was actually intent upon stopping me.

"Monty, that's what bathroom rugs are for."

"But this isn't a bathroom rug, it's just carpet. It isn't rubberized. Mother doesn't like it to get wet."

These were the sorts of conversations in which Monty and I did actually engage. There was no stopping him when he decided to resolve a mindless issue.

"Turn off the water then, and I'll dry off in here," I told him.

"No, then I'll get cold."

"Well, what do you want me to do?"

I asked this as a way of pointing out the idiocy of the

discussion, but I came to understand very quickly that it had been the wrong question.

"Just wait for me. I want you to stay until I'm through," Monty said briskly, clearly pleased to have been asked. "You can sit over there."

He waved grandly at the corner of the very large shower stall. He waved again with a little flourish.

And I obeyed. I was so reluctant that my body seemed to lag behind my legs, the way babies' bodies do when they're learning to walk, but I did it. I sat in the corner and slid down so that I could hide my face against my knees, since that made my humiliation easier to bear.

I obeyed because I didn't know how to assert myself, and because the groundbreaking thoughts I'd been having—that Monty and I could relate to each other as human beings—were fragile and easily overwhelmed. Monty had made it clear that even if he was just a man, he was still the man in charge, and the opportunity for new intimacy was lost.

And as the months went by, the prospect became truly buried. As must be the case when mates are playing roles instead of searching for each other, the point of our marriage soon became to manipulate each other so that we could each have what we wanted. I believe that I became particularly adept at this, since I was smarter. Monty was actually a fairly simple fellow to maneuver around. I remember that there was a specific day, a third milestone in our marriage, when I realized I understood my part in our relationship at last.

It was the day of my first shopping spree. I had always loved clothes, and my mother had always spoiled me, but this was the first time since I'd married that I'd allowed myself to have anything new, since Monty's financial code had proved to be very consistent and had even outlawed the possibility of our installing a phone over the summer. Then in the fall, when he'd enrolled at the University of Utah and had more to occupy him, he began to relax a little. When he began appearing occasionally with a couple of thick steaks, when he sprang for a nicer shirt than he'd ever owned before, when he admitted he was glad that I'd convinced him to move to an upgraded apartment, I felt as grateful to him for appreciating our few indulgences as I would have if he'd had anything to do with providing them. I knew that I was getting ready to fly through the window created by his new behavior.

We had moved to Salt Lake City after our wedding, and the store I went to that day was Makoff's, a chic, quiet shaft of rooms with thick carpets on one of the city's main streets. It was filled with the long midi-skirts that were popular then, and the smart vests, and racks of dressing gowns including the one I couldn't resist—a rust-colored velvet robe that draped luxuriously and cinched me in at the waist. I was so crazy about it that as I watched the salesgirl shroud it in rustling paper I was sorry to see it disappear. I drove home with it unwrapped and spread full length across the other seat, as though it were a passenger.

And then I cleaned. We were living in the Lower Avenues, a quaint neighborhood that bordered downtown, and our apartment was a sunny one filled with the inoffensive blond furniture from the fifties that's found in thrift stores. I had personalized it with dried-flower pictures in gilt frames, with huge bunches of hot-pink glass grapes, with woolen afghans crocheted in bright colors, and with the other objets d'art that I had created at meetings of the women's auxiliary. I considered our apartment a beautiful place and I always kept it tidy, but now I scrubbed it with new vigor, determined that a whiff of disinfectant would assault Monty on his way in the door. There was to be no room for personal criticisms that night beyond the issue of my extravagance.

Finally I set to work on the way *I* was looking. As our marriage had progressed, I'd become unsure whether Monty was attracted to me or my dowry, but I wasn't going to risk leaving anything undone. I singed my long hair with the curling iron and broke out the eyeshadow, and right at the end I swathed myself in the elegant new robe, the one that had cost fifty dollars. Then I waited, perched agitatedly on the edge of the tufted turquoise sofa and fingering the pearl choker at my throat.

Our apartment was at the head of a single flight of stairs. When I heard the first-floor door swoosh open, I went to stand on the top step. I saw Monty come around the curve in the staircase, saw his eyes light first on the robe's long skirt that was all he could see without lifting his head. I was pulling on my necklace so hard that I thought I might rip it off. By the time he was standing fully in front of me I could see that his face was stern. And then I let fly with my line.

"I know it's the most expensive thing on the menu, but I want it anyway, please, honey," I said.

When he finally smiled at me, I knew it was a turning point in the marriage.

III

Once I learned to negotiate there was far less friction, but ours was only a surface calm. My deftness couldn't remedy a profoundly dreadful fit. I felt the gears miss most painfully when we were with other couples, when I thought everyone else might see him through my eyes, and so I hated to socialize with anyone whose approval I wanted. Sometimes we would visit Monty's brother, Winston, and the two of them would become greatly caught up in the discussion of drugstore prices of which they never seemed to tire. I would watch them animatedly exchanging information about Neo-Synephrine on sale and be glad we were only with Winston, who didn't see as I did that Monty's interests were coma-inducing. I didn't want any new friends.

Which left me with a lot of time for housekeeping. It had to be housekeeping, since I'd dropped out of school when I'd married and hadn't looked for a job. We didn't need the money, and like the vast majority of the young Mormon women I knew, I believed that God wanted me at home. I didn't mind the limitation: I was so loath to expose myself to people that I felt the sort of gratitude toward my heritage that you feel for any very good excuse that saves you. I set out to perfect my "calling" as a homemaker.

I was not aided in this endeavor by early training or natural talent. A vehemence for order had not been instilled in me by my high-living mother, who had relied on hired help when I was growing up. I possessed very few practical skills to apply to the bucketful of bottled soaps and spray polishes that some unfanciful soul had sent to us as a wedding present.

And so, while we were visiting Monty's parents that first summer, I placed myself in my mother-in-law's hands. Meticulous and energetic, Amelia Brown vibrated among her tasks like a small, excellent engine. She was a genius in matters of shortcutting and organization, as well as a master chef, but in my eyes her most reassuring quality was her boundless confidence. Her judgments about what constituted a well-kept home and a poorly managed one were absolute; she didn't understand the concept of interpretation. I could relax completely under her tutelage, certain that by mimicking her housekeeping strategies exactly I stood to become a paragon in her eyes, and thus in Monty's.

Amelia counseled that if I rinsed the breakfast dishes thoroughly and arranged them symmetrically in the sink, on rubber mats, it was acceptable to leave them unwashed until lunchtime. She taught me to flip broiling meat only once. She schooled me in shaking the living-room curtains to loosen the dust from them before I vacuumed, and in tending the magnificent crystal she had presented to us at the wedding. At her behest, I sorted the household drawers in our little apartment every single week; I made a file of her recipes and kept sponging the file off. Remembering and enforcing all of Amelia's rules took a great deal of time, even though our apartment was small. I somehow became competent enough to comply, however, even though I am now the sort of housekeeper who stands in front of a cupboard that needs straightening and can only feel confused.

I also tried to nurture my marriage by developing a network of advisers—my bishop, my brother, and my shrink. I couldn't hear enough about what others thought would improve my life with Monty, particularly if those "others" were the men whom I recognized as the voices of authority. I desperately wanted someone to teach me to be happily married.

Once my three advisers were in place, my daily routine began to resemble that of the characters in daytime TV soap operas, where no one's job interferes with a schedule of endless visits to the houses of friends and enemies in pursuit of invariably grave discourse. I literally went from one to the other, an empty receptacle seeking enlightenment.

In the case of Bishop Miles Rector, enlightenment never came, but not because he didn't try. He was a thirtyish, bespectacled, matter-of-fact high school science teacher with no neck, the sort of man who believed that if you kept your eyes on your responsibilities and didn't brood too much, God would bless you with some form of contentment. He gave to me unstintingly of his time, and his manner with me was well-meaning but entirely brusque.

"What are you trying to tell me—that you're afraid to make anything of yourself because you think you'll show Monty up, and then hate him?" he barked at me crossly during one of our innumerable counseling sessions, when I was coming close to exploring with him some more reasons for my reclusiveness. He said it as though nothing could be more ridiculous. And although I *was* trying to tell him that, I immediately denied it. I was rarely able to express my true feelings to Bishop Rector because I thought my true feelings about Monty were ungodly.

Even though I couldn't confide in Bishop Rector, even though he had no transforming advice to offer me, on a hundred different days I scanned his face with an intensity that would have unnerved him if he'd been a more sensitive man. I thought that because God inspired him, everything he was telling me was significant but I just couldn't interpret him correctly.

Sometimes when I left Bishop Rector, I drove into Provo. Or, if he could be convinced to make the trip to town, my brother Len came to me. When we couldn't get together we talked endlessly on the phone. Len was completing his bachelor's degree at BYU that year and living in the same apartment that he and Monty had once shared. Because the apartment was still crowded with roommates, when I called, Len would drag the phone out his front door for privacy, and would pace on the bathmat-sized stoop for hours in numbing winter weather, his viewpoints forming clouds of frost around his head.

He was becoming a man of rigid values; he was even choosing clothes that grew by degrees stiffer and less imaginative. Where once he had favored suede coats and smart boots, he had worn since his mission ended a variety of meticulously pressed shirts in dim colors, and unclamorous V-necked sweaters in maroon and navy. He kept his hair cut unfashionably short, he said because of his enrollment in the National Guard. Most affectingly, he had begun to carry himself so that his sternness, which in the beginning of his adult life had come and gone as a mask for his shyness, had become a genuine hallmark. He tended to start sentences directed at me by speaking my name with a schoolmaster's emphasis. *"Deb-*orah! Sometimes you try to *cas*trate your husband!" is the sort of thing he would cry agitatedly, I thought with some accuracy. His bias during all of our talks was very clear: He thought my marriage should endure at all costs, and he thought I was the problem within it.

It would be hard to overstate the extent to which I had loved my brother all my life, and loved him then, and took him seriously. I admired him with the senseless sense of inferiority that characterized all my dealings with men. And as my little marriage whimpered and roiled, I looked to him for wisdom, believing that at age twenty-three and with far less experience with love than even I possessed, he would reveal to me the key elements of a joyful union, because of his priesthood. In fact, I had always trusted the clairvoyance of his priesthood much farther than my own husband's, since I had been trusting Len's dealings with God for longer. Len rewarded me with unstinting advice and wrathful disapproval that would persist for ten long years.

My psychiatrist was the third stop on my advice-seeking rounds. I didn't choose him because he was a compassionate listener who could bring the wavy lines of my marriage into focus, however. Instead, my goal was to find a physician whom no one in the Salt Lake City church community would fault me for, if that were possible.

A Mormon distrust lay over the entire matter of psychotherapy. The thing you heard from church leaders was that a doctor mired in science rather than spirituality might try to supplant God's laws with his own. (The thing you didn't hear was that people become far less compliant once they've examined their true feelings and blossomed into freethinkers.) When my bishop had recognized his limitations in trying to wrestle with my snarled emotions, I had asked him to refer me to an entirely devout counselor, and he had pointed the way to Dr. Johnson, whose unequivocal qualification was that he was very distantly related to one of the highest leaders of the church.

Dr. Johnson's style of therapy was to impress upon me the acceptable ways in which good church members conduct their marriages. Repeatedly and with visible vanity running his hand through his roof of bright red hair, he had used his own marriage to illustrate these points. One example of perfect, church-sanctioned marriage found Dr. Johnson awakening with his wife, who even at daybreak was overwhelmingly weary with her thirteenth pregnancy, and never complaining as she nuzzled into his shoulder in obvious need of comforting that her terrible breath was asphyxiating him. "She is a *good* woman, a devoted wife and mother, and she deserves my support. I was happy to control myself in order to give it to her," he told me in a frenzy of sanctimonious self-congratulation.

For a long time the many hours I spent with Dr. Johnson were as entirely without value as those with Bishop Rector, and for the same reason. I couldn't be honest with him—or with myself—because I was far too aware of how I *should* feel. If I confessed that I was simply bored beyond imagining with my dull husband and tired of his demands, that on most days my fondest wish was for him to vanish irrevocably into the twisted heart of a car wreck, wouldn't I appear to be less than a perfect helpmeet and partner? And on another level, my reticence was an even more deeply rooted problem than the reluctance to be judged. Spouting the party line came so naturally to me that I didn't know I was doing it. So I didn't know to quit.

IV

Despite his limitations, Dr. Johnson was destined to endure in memory as a great mentor, seeing as how he was the first to point to a place in my body and soul that was truly my own. I'm sure he didn't mean to.

We were talking about my sex life one day, and I was lamenting the fact that it was emotionless and devoid of climaxes where I was concerned, something that surprised me after the easy orgasms of courtship.

"Do you ever *masturbate* to orgasm?" Dr. Johnson asked. He wore contacts, and as he spoke he was engaging in a spasm of eyelid fluttering that distracted me and kept me from hearing him for a few seconds. The interval created a little vacuum that the force and significance of his words then exploded into.

He had spoken completely without judgment. Could he really be suggesting that masturbation was a harmless pastime? Dr. Johnson, the man of God?

To say the least, the church was hostile toward masturbation: The practice was viewed as a playground slide that led straight to hell. Directed to young men, as though only they could be tempted, church teachings relating to masturbation were perhaps most unforgettably immortalized in a pamphlet written by a respected church leader during my adolescence, wherein he counseled young men in strategies that would help them to resist their urges. In order to not masturbate, he advised them to reduce the amount of spice in their diets, to tie their hands to the bed frame so they wouldn't reach to mindlessly masturbate while in a "semi-sleep condition," and to pray. "But when you pray, don't pray about this problem, for that will tend to keep it in your mind more than ever," he advised them.

So Dr. Johnson's easy tolerance was a bombshell. I was still reeling from the impact when the aftershock hit me—*masturbation could end in orgasm*.

This was an entirely unexpected wrinkle. I had never comprehended the appeal of masturbation because I had misunderstood it to be nothing more than a way to experience the beginning stages of arousal. I'd had no idea it could propel you along all the way to the end. Now I sat before Dr. Johnson knowing that for the first time he had truly changed my life.

I left the session in a happy daze of anticipation and drove home to an apartment that I was delighted to find empty. There I threw myself onto the bed, on my stomach, luxuriating in my aloneness. I masturbated to orgasm still wearing all my clothing and my shoes. It took only a couple of minutes and it was delicious. How I loved not feeling nerve-racked by a need to clamber back into my garments, loved not trying to force waves of passion to rise above my dread at being with Monty. Afterward I could feel every nerve ending I possessed.

In the weeks that followed, I discovered my body and my sexuality for the first time. I was a girl whose understanding of the place of sex in life had been determined by frozen-faced prophets, and yet I slipped easily and without guilt into a happy obsession with my imagined, sensuous worlds.

When intent upon "masturbating to orgasm"—the phrase that began to play in my mind like a mantra—I could find a place within myself that was out of reach of the counsel of my elders, and that knew there was nothing harmful in my gifts to myself. This permission to feel pleasure seemed to radiate out of a sure, pure center where values were universal and timeless and never damning. For a long time I didn't realize that this core of my personality could also transform the parts of my life that weren't sexual.

The main gratification of those times was not metaphysical, however; it had everything to do with the physical. It was while I was "masturbating to orgasm" that I felt the strength of my long legs, my vital blood and brain, the reality of my youth. I could think that I was longer than the bed, could experience my breath filling my lungs as though it were a flavor. Sometimes afterward I would run my fingertips along the inside of my other arm, or behind one of my knees or across a nipple that even through a sweater could not have been more alive to touch if the outer flesh had been rubbed away. I would know that my skin covered every crease of my body with sensation, that it did not just flare up occasionally into a pair of lips or a clitoris that could record pleasure.

This was a completely new form of knowledge. The teachings of my youth had been so focused on mysticism and the spirit that the body had been discussed only as a package to house the part of me that was eternal. It had never occurred to me before that my body was *me*. It was like discovering a twin; my body seemed that separate from the part of me that I thought I knew. But finding it was a beginning, and over the next fifteen years I would slowly merge with it.

Finding it was also an almost unqualified pleasure. There was only one painful moment, and that was when sensation and thought unfortunately collided. I was running my fingers lightly over my face following an orgasm, and I stopped in mid-stroke, halted by a question that paralyzed me with fear: *Is this the only joy I will ever feel?*

I was not in the habit of peering into the future, not because I was avoiding it but because when I'd gotten married I'd thought everything about the future had been settled. Monty and I would work in the church auxiliaries, we'd have kids. Now this unexpected thing had happened—this masturbation thing—that had opened me up to unimagined depths of feeling, and I was realizing that there could be many experiences ahead that I hadn't foreseen. What else would cause me pleasure and pain? How else was I going to change? How else was life going to?

It was a profoundly disorienting moment, a sensation of the complete loss of order in the world. And once I'd glimpsed chaos I could never again recover the bedrock certainty of a preordained life. The possibility of ambush was always there, nibbling at my brain, so I tried to numb it. And where the act of masturbation had been the thing that revealed me to myself, it now became the thing that hid me. I masturbated constantly; I became an orgasm machine.

Sometimes after dinner, when Monty could be counted on to remain in the bathroom for a few minutes, I'd sneak into the bedroom for another stolen climax, one meant to distract me from the doldrums of those evenings. One day when I'd motored down the street a few miles to the soup bar at the elegant Hotel Utah, which was a favorite lunchtime haunt of mine, I slipped into the ladies' restroom on my way out and masturbated while leaning against the inside of the tin wall of the farthest stall.

I grew very possessive of my right to masturbate and very cranky when it was denied me. Once when Monty's parents were in town for a week and we'd been socializing with them for several evenings in a row, I begged off one night so that I could have some time alone. I knew they thought it was because I was embarrassed by the faltering state of my marriage, and I was content for them to think that. It was even partially true; Monty had confided to them in front of me that I was always running in for counseling sessions with the bishop, or was always running over to be propped up by Dr. Johnson. I had hated the fact that they knew.

But the bigger reason was that I wanted to masturbate to orgasm. I invented an excuse and drove out to Cottonwood Mall, a long tunnel of gray shops in south Salt Lake. I spent a miserable evening wandering from store to store, just waiting for the moment when I could trust that Monty and his family had cleared out of our apartment and gone to dinner.

I drove home slowly, during the last half hour of a heavy snowfall. The thick winter sky was hanging so low that I had the feeling I was inching down a tube, and the crystalline streets were nearly deserted. On the narrow streets in the Lower Avenues, fresh snowdrifts made by the city's plows were banked up on both sides, but already the roads were coated and crunchy again. The world seems to be a very private place when its parts are obscured by snow, and it may have been because of that sense of isolation that I didn't wait to get home. Several blocks away from our apartment, I decided to masturbate to orgasm on the spot.

I swerved into a snowdrift and stopped the car, then clambered into the Camaro's stunted backseat. There was only room for half of me back there; I scrunched up on my stomach like an inchworm. And then, of course, I began to pursue my goal, navigating through many layers of insulating winter clothes. I was completely absorbed, and had gotten pretty far along, when I realized that the car door had been wrenched open behind me. I swiveled my head around, panic-stricken, but was unable on such short notice to flip over in the sardine-can space, so I was still lying on my stomach with my hand pinned under me in the moment when I saw who it was.

Amelia Brown was standing framed in the car-door opening. Her pretty reddish hair, which she wore cut short and curly, was rapidly being covered with feathery snow. Behind her, my father-in-law, Freddie, was crouching down so he could peer into the car over her shoulder. Both their faces were screwed into classic expressions of annoyance and concern, the sort my own parents had worn on days when I'd announced I was too sick to go to school and they hadn't known whether I was lying.

"Debbie . . . honey, are you all right?" Amelia wanted to know. At least she said something like that. I was too busy trying to roll onto my back as nonchalantly as I could to take note of the exact wording.

"Yes, I'm fine. Yes," I said.

"None of us was in the mood for dinner, so we're on the way back to the hotel. We knew this was your car."

"Yes, it is," I agreed, eager to establish a rapport.

"Well, you shouldn't be out here in the cold," she said. "I know things are difficult at home, but you should go back to the apartment."

"I will," I promised.

"Have you been crying?" she asked. "You're all flushed."

"I, I feel like I *might* cry."

"Well, no matter how tense things are between you and Monty right now, you can't lie around in your car in the street."

"No, it isn't helping," I agreed.

"So will you go home now?"

"Yes."

They left me alone then. And when they had gone, I finished.

Five

I

I was not the first person to find a fluttering independence within my sexuality or to discover that it wasn't independence enough. I was still a long way from knowing that I should direct my own life. I had not claimed enough of myself to even take the measure of my own despair. I needed someone to point out my misery to me—a coconspirator in depression—and I found one in my old friend Hannie.

Hannie had been my roommate at BYU before she had married Dickie Gardiner and conceived their first child. At college, she was a beautiful girl with a nearly constantly rosy face and the sort of weighty, wavy, caramel-colored hair that guaranteed the world would require nothing more from her appearance. She also possessed an intellectual side that was unprecedented among my girlfriends: One of her wedding presents to me had been a much-read paperback copy of Joyce's *The Portrait of the Artist as a Young Man*. I had always thought she was destined for unusual things. I'd been very surprised when, by marrying Dickie, she'd done the usual.

I was also surprised by her choice of Dickie himself, a fellow with little to recommend him in terms of personal charm. He was a smart, sober returned missionary who absolutely never kidded around, who was intent on becoming a public-sector lawyer, a prosecutor. On the few occasions when Hannie and I got together with our husbands, he parked his stocky frame in our living room and shared with Monty his feelings about having law and order at home and in the world. These feelings were not very complex—Dickie was *for* law and order—but he nonetheless delivered them again and again, as though the nuances couldn't easily be gleaned.

I couldn't imagine why Hannie had married him, but I never said so directly, since I didn't want to hear her pose a similar question to me. Then she volunteered one day that she had prayed about it and had felt impressed that marrying Dickie was the right thing. She said, in a really tired way, that she still believed God sanctioned her marriage.

Our lives were similar, although Hannie's was actually worse. Where my marriage was a washout, a matter of insensitivity and cylinders missing, Hannie's was a tyrannical ordeal. She didn't enjoy sex very much, and so Dickie read aloud to her in bed from sex manuals he'd checked out at the university library, as though the key to passion was memorizing the precise names for genitalia. Hannie said that, if she seemed to be dozing, Dickie would read aloud and bounce up and down on the mattress at the same time. She told me that once, when she fell asleep anyway, he took her by her shoulders and pushed her skull sharply into the headboard. Another time he dragged her up the stairs to their apartment because she had been about to leave for a movie rather than spend an intimate evening with him.

She said to me, in a muted voice I'd never heard before, "I can't tell you how it feels that this man who is supposed to take me to heaven might beat me up." I believe that he never really did, but that the prospect, unfounded or not, always lay between them.

I began going over to Hannie's almost daily, to lounge on her dingy rented sofas and to swig soda out of wedding-present glasses. I was aware that we both possessed in spades everything we were supposed to want, everything that God wanted for us, everything that filled with content the other young wives we knew. I also knew that by virtue of being already pregnant, Hannie possessed even more than I did, but that she wasn't holding up very well. There wasn't much color in her cheeks anymore and her hair had become so limp and faded that it looked bleached. She had taken to holding it back with an elastic—no ribbon, no barrette—so that the uneven ends were always bunched together, an announcement that she'd given up on haircuts. Even her marvelous, wry chatter had slowed down.

It was only when I was staring into the face of her unhappiness, knowing that she wasn't a whiner, that I could feel I deserved my own pain. Moments when I knew it were the only authentic ones in the day, when my mind and emotions truly fit inside my body.

One of the things we did again and again was page through old issues of church magazines, *The Improvement Era* and *The Ensign,* searching for the marriage advice from General Authorities that was regularly published there. Hannie never threw these magazines away and her collection extended back more than ten years, so that if we'd been tuned in to it, we could have noticed that our church leaders were addressing the prospects of marriage and divorce with increasing panic as sex roles across the nation began to loosen. In 1964, President David O. McKay was urging men and women, "No other success can compensate for failure in the home," an encouraging maxim that was still relatively unalarmed. By late 1972, when Hannie and I were searching for answers, the rhetoric had heightened, at least partially in response to feminism.

We found a warning of McKay's, for instance, that was intended especially for women, and that to me seemed aimed at the foul heart of my own restlessness: ". . . Any woman who will break up her home because of some selfish desire . . . is also untrue to the covenants she has made in the house of the Lord." Another General Authority, James Cullimore, had written the previous year that "divorce is usually the result of one or both not living the gospel," an admonition that, as I read it to Hannie, filled me inexplicably with shame. Perhaps most affectingly, we came across an address written by Thomas Monson, a General Authority who has continued to rise in the ranks in the decades since and who will probably become the church's president one day. It was titled "Women's Movement: Liberation or Deception?," and Hannie and I managed to believe it suggested that we were suffering in loveless marriages for particularly excellent reasons.

". . . So long as Mormon women cling to the simple ideal of home and joyous family life, so long as they feel the measure of their creation is homemaker . . . so long is the Church and the nation safe," wrote Monson. He labeled liberated women, the pursuers of personal freedom and careers, as "the Pied Pipers of sin who have led women away from the divine role of womanhood down the pathway of error," and encouraged women everywhere to accept three major challenges for the seventies: "Sustain your husband. . . . Strengthen your home. . . . Serve your God." If women found themselves feeling unappreciated as they pursued these invisible tasks, he offered what he must have believed was comforting proof that their families held them in high regard, but his vague anecdote made me very uneasy, even at the time: "I think [your families] do appreciate you. One of the questions after a study of magnets at one junior high school was, 'What begins with M and picks things up?' The obvious answer was 'magnet.' However, more than a third of the students answered 'mother.' "

The message was actually a little skewed for Hannie and me. We didn't want to escape marriage and become careerists: Underneath it all, we just wanted different marriages from the ones we had. Nonetheless, while I was reading Monson's remarks, I had a flash of relief that I'd dismissed my post-wedding day histrionics to my mother. For probably the last time, I was glad I'd stayed married to Monty.

Hannie and I began doing our grocery shopping together. Wretched with morning sickness, she would stand eternally in the shower, as though she were slowly gaining the strength to move from the needling spray. Then she would dress and we would drive to Albertson's.

One day we wound through the aisles loading our carts with ground beef and the other paraphernalia of casseroles. We were reminiscing about BYU—swapping stories that, only eight or nine months after they had happened, were already as distant to me as childhood. I had made an effort with my appearance that day, something that I did less and less, and I caught my reflection in the shiny glass doors of the dairy section. Like Hannie's, my long hair was pulled back into a ponytail, and unlike her, I had swabbed on lipstick that morning that was rather startlingly red. I was wearing vivid yellow cotton trousers and a stark-white shirt.

I should have been a familiar, innocuous sight, but I wasn't. I was strangely transformed: The bright colors I was wearing seemed to overshadow me completely. My face, particularly my eyes, was so obscured by my clothes and makeup that its contours had vanished.

I looked closer into the glass, trying to bring myself into

sharper relief, but saw instead that Hannie was standing just behind my shoulder, listlessly awaiting her own chance at a milk carton and possessing no more vitality than a watercolor. I glanced back and forth between her physical presence and her wan reflection and could not find my stomach when I realized that one was not much more powerful than the other.

We were only girls, and the high point of our day was a trip to the grocery store, and we were fading. It was the sequence of events I had always expected for myself—marriage and a descent into dailyness—and yet I was shocked to experience my own slow disappearance. Suddenly I grasped sickeningly that false measures of resuscitation like masturbation weren't going to even come close anymore to filling the emptiness I'd been trying so desperately to ignore.

The room began to reel, and I shoved my arm out full length, the palm pressed flat against the dairy-case door with such force that when I finally removed my hand, my fingerprints on the glass were nearly as distinct as paint. If Hannie hadn't slipped her arm around me to steady me, I'm not sure that I wouldn't have simply keeled over.

Instead, I said something like this to her: "I know that I can't leave Monty, but I've just realized I don't know how to stay, either. I don't know how to hang on."

II

I had crossed a perilous line, had finally recognized I didn't possess the strength or perhaps the insensitivity that would allow me to burrow more deeply into a role that didn't bring me any joy.

I began to abandon the pretext of being a good wife. I quit getting up early enough to make Monty's breakfast, began keeping my eyes closed while he hunted around in the bedroom for his socks and shirts and sprayed himself with antiperspirant so pungent that I couldn't avoid flaring my nostrils a little as I feigned sleep. I could feel the weight of his presence in the room like a barbell lying across my chest.

I couldn't get out to the market for groceries on a schedule, couldn't get a meat loaf into the oven even when I had managed to bring food into the house. Usually Monty would return from campus in the late afternoons and find me still in bed, the apartment strewn with newspapers and with recipes torn jaggedly out of *Good Housekeeping* that never found their way into the recipe file anymore. He would stand in the bedroom doorway and peer into the gloom I'd created by tacking blankets over the thin bedroom curtains. His eyes would search for me, a lump in the bed, and when he had found me he would slam the bedroom door, consigning us to separate parts of the house with an angry bang.

I quit showing up for my piano lessons, quit the women's auxiliary, quit sliding into Monty's arms on the occasions when he and his condom climbed into bed at night, still willing to make their chilly imprint inside me. At first I cried a good deal, aimlessly, shut away in the small dim bedroom, but after a while I even quit that. I began dozing for most of the day. Sometimes I would move out to the couch in the living room as though that would help me stay awake and amount to something, and then I would doze there.

I was getting as close to death as I could, since I could allow myself to leave Monty only if convinced I would actually die by staying with him. The threat of death seemed an excuse God might accept, the way I had always heard He would not censure abortion if the life of the mother was at stake.

Unaware that I had come into the world in order to make choices, I had finally made the first lonely choice of my life that day at Albertson's. But in order to appease God for daring to make it, I would have to pay a still higher price of agony and fear before I carried through.

The suicide attempt, when it came, wasn't well thought out or effective, and, worst of all, wasn't entirely convincing. As Monty propelled me out the front door to the hospital, I remember thinking that Dr. Johnson and the other people whom I'd been begging for the answers to a satisfactory life would have to realize now that I needed them to come up with something more.

I was able to walk to the car because I had tried to kill myself only a few minutes before in full view of Monty, who'd been reading the morning paper in the living room. In a bottle the size of a coffee mug, I had possessed a bounteous supply of tranquilizers given to me by the family doctor when I had left for college. I had not been much tempted by sedatives at BYU, but that day long after I shoved literal handfuls into my mouth and gagged elaborately while standing in the hallway. My gestures were so frantic and clumsy that I also sprayed the gleaming pills all over the floor. Our regimens for living had disintegrated by then to the point that neither Monty nor I ever swept them up. After a while they got mashed into split, slick casings and white powder and were ground into the taupey carpet.

At the emergency room, someone ushered me into a curtained cubicle and gave me ipecac in a cup small enough to be cupped in my palm. It was plenty of ipecac, though. After I had vomited Librium into a pan, Monty came to stand at the foot of the bed, his arms crossed on his chest. The walls and the floor and the curtains were very white, and in the midst of all that coolness he was throwing off so much angry heat that he could have been a red hot poker. Drowsy and defenseless, I was taking him in as though he knew everything about me. His parents were in town again that week, and the main thing he said to me was "I know you only did this to ruin my parents' vacation." He had lost patience with me long before.

Beyond the curtains I could hear swift feet and raised voices attending to someone who'd just been pulled out of a car wreck. My temples pounded with a headache that seemed to be forcing my eyes out of the sockets. And what I was thinking was "It's all right that Monty is fed up with me, since I'm going to be leaving anyway." I thought it listlessly, as though for the thousandth time, and as dispassionately as though it were something Dr. Johnson had recommended instead of my heart's desire. I had been preparing for the thought in a million ways.

To make sure there was no danger, they kept me in the hospital for a half-dozen hours. At some point Dr. Johnson charged into my little cubicle, and even through my heavy-lidded eyes I could see that his expression was only slightly more sympathetic than my husband's. Once back in our apartment, sleeping it off interminably in my bedroom refuge, I surfaced a couple of times with the clearly formed thought that I would be facing the future alone.

Yet I somehow shifted into high gear. In the days following the Librium binge I functioned like a homing pigeon, setting out to reach a destination for reasons that had nothing to do with rational thinking. There was a sense of inevitability to everything I attempted—to the swift motions of my arms as I reached to pack our blue-flowered dishes while Monty was at school, to the pile of skirts and shirts and socks that grew on the closet floor while I sorted through my clothes, determining what could be thrown away before I moved, I assumed back to Florida. I wasn't calm as I readied myself for divorce, or even frank about it—at first I told Monty that I was storing some dishes because of a lack of shelf space, and indulging myself in spring cleaning. But I kept going.

I did tell Hannie that I was leaving. She was fairly supportive, in the mild way that had become her hallmark. She even suggested a reason for my new determination: "You've had a year to realize what your life with Monty is actually going to be like. It was just fear before, and you were able to believe you might be wrong." She thought I was enabled by desperation, as I did.

In the years since, I have begun to wonder what desperation really signals, though. I think that in some cases, and certainly in this one, it is an encouraging word sent by the part of the soul we can't reach that knows what's good for us. Maybe the message is cloaked as a misery because only pain makes us willing to change.

I think that when I left Monty I was guided by something more sure-footed than instinct—an unconscious understanding that finally empowered me to fly in the face of my church leaders' advice and my family's teachings and my own beliefs about what constituted a respectable life. My soul knew the path to a broader perspective, and knew that I wasn't ready for a partnership with a man. It was pulling me away from Monty so that I could try to finish growing up alone.

III

Monty didn't go out of my life painlessly, but he did go quickly. It was my father who found the jet-propelled lawyer who forced the divorce through in two mere weeks, as though I'd gone to Reno. Dad had flown out to Utah as soon as Monty slammed the door behind him for the final time, and he spent the two weeks before I went to court holed up with me in my little apartment. At first, I found this to be very nerve-racking, because I'd never spent much time with my distant father—his career in the insurance business had kept him on the road throughout my childhood. I was also feeling very self-conscious about my situation; I had figured Dad would be full of judgments now that my marriage was really over.

To my surprise, divorce turned out to be instead another of those realms, like birth control, in which my stern father easily turned a deaf ear to the harpings of the General Authorities. He treated my divorce as though it were nothing more willful than a terrible car accident for which the other guy had been cited, accepting it with sorrow but never a word of rebuke.

Once or twice he even put his arms around me while we were sitting together on the sofa and I was feeling a deep, deep weariness creeping over me, settling onto my face with a sensation of such permanence that it could have been age. He held me and rocked me slightly, an activity that he and I had engaged in very little in my lifetime and hardly ever would again. For the first time I realized that it was more important to him that I be happy than that I remain married to Monty. Since this sentiment was coming from my father, the symbol of all that was godly in the world, I wondered whether divorce was something I might even be forgiven for one day.

My divorce from Monty took place on Valentine's Day, only nine months after the wedding.

I drove alone to the courthouse in the center of town and endured a brief list of questions posed by the world-weary, graying judge. He spoke so quickly and in a voice so fossilized by boredom that I was not completely sure I heard the last question correctly.

"If your husband said, 'Deborah, I love you, I want you back,' would you go back?" the judge wanted to know.

When I said I wouldn't, he declared me to be divorced. "Don't get married again before eight-thirty tomorrow morning," he said tonelessly.

And that shocked me. With the first flush of public defensiveness about divorce, which would soon become familiar to me, I hoped that nothing about *my* attitude had brought the remark on. I hoped he knew that I had not filed for divorce on a whim.

"Excuse me, but are you a member of the church?" I asked him very politely. In Utah there are innumerable religions, but only one church. I was ready to identify myself with it and to launch into a monologue about my belief in the importance of marriage.

"Young lady, I can't imagine how it would benefit you to know," the judge said, and he looked down at his next sheaf of papers.

I walked out into the brilliant morning, where sunlight was reflecting off snowdrifts that were just beginning to lose their sharp outlines to the warmth of the day. The city was still very bright, not yet soiled with the gray snow that wept into curbside gullies as one of the first signs of spring. I felt clean, too, almost weak, as though from a very hot bath. I realized without surprise that I didn't miss Monty. At that moment, the sensation of not missing him was as piercing as missing him would have been.

In the months and years ahead, I never missed him. The memory of his presence slid out of my thinking as easily as though it were egg white. As I stood facing into the sun for the first time as a free woman, I already knew that was how it would be.

Six

I

In the early seventies I engaged in a battle for my civil rights against a hierarchy of gentlemen who were determined to hold my history against me as fully as though it were a scandalous one. I was humiliated by this persecution—which I couldn't quickly recognize as persecution, because I believed at first that I was guilty of something.

I couldn't think otherwise. By 1973 a small population of Mormon women was beginning to experiment with consciousness-raising and the concepts of feminism, but I had never met any of them. I possessed no context for the outrages that began occurring the year after Monty and I separated, and I couldn't wonder whether Monty was being treated any differently from me in divorce's aftermath. I didn't think in terms of deliberate discrimination, and although it doesn't begin to excuse them, I don't think my church leaders did, either. What happened to me as a divorcée—the ordeal of accusations and threats that wore me down until I was tissue-thin—had nothing like conscious thought behind it. The struggle was automatic, both for those who spearheaded my spiritual rehabilitation and for me. We were all complete products of our culture.

The most powerful condemnation came from the Gen-

eral Authorities, in that, once I was divorced, I was required
to write to them often about sex. My hometown bishop,
Bishop Pruitt, gave me the assignment of the letters. I had
taken refuge in my parents' Florida house following the divorce, and Bishop Pruitt visited me there as a one-man church
tribunal. He sat in a frilly pink chair in my private parlor, and,
because temple marriage is such a serious matter to Mormons,
he asked to know the reasons why mine had not survived.

This inquiry placed me at something of a loss. I couldn't
imagine saying to a kindly, slightly distracted engineer who
was also my spiritual leader: "I felt so trapped there, as though
my life had ended." I couldn't imagine that such an explana-
tion would be regarded as a very good excuse. I rambled on
about little arguments that Monty and I had had until Bishop
Pruitt stopped me. "I think we can say that your divorce was
the result of inadequate preparation for marriage," he said.

Which didn't mean my youthful error could be overlooked: Bishop Pruitt explained that he would have to rescind
my temple recommend. It was the church's standard response
to divorce and a very symbolic one, since the privilege of
templegoing was only for the worthy. Despite Bishop Pruitt's
completely innocent evaluation of my marriage's unraveling,
divorce had transformed me into a woman strongly suspected
by the General Authorities of sleeping around; they apparently
couldn't imagine that anything short of sexual sin could lead
to dissolution. In order to requalify for a temple recommend
I would need to convince the General Authorities otherwise by
describing my sexual activities to them very exactly in a series
of letters. I experienced this exercise of Bishop Pruitt's as the
equivalent of writing "I am not a virgin anymore" several
hundred times on a blackboard, in front of everyone I had ever
known.

Despite my embarrassment, I really threw my heart into the letters. I still have the rough drafts, only somewhat smudged with cramped lines of penciled rewrites trailing into the margins, and they are chilling in their naked longing for absolution from the man I trusted most in the world, who possessed the magic to cleanse me.

"Dear President Spencer Kimball, My bishop has suggested that I write again to you and emphasize that at no time previous to my marriage, and at no time since my divorce, have I had sexual relations, and at no time during my marriage was I unfaithful to my husband," I wrote in the last letter, more than eighteen months after the divorce was final. "I have remained constant in this regard and I am striving in every way to live the Gospel. The Gospel matters so much to me, and I want to find my proper place within it again. I know that I can do it, with your help. Thank you for your kind attention and concern. It's comforting to know you're there."

I believed that the president of the Mormon Church was reading my letters, and I was only a little hurt that he never replied. I understood that he was very busy.

Even beyond the humiliation of the letters I felt my impurity keenly. One day, worshiping again in the Clearwater chapel I'd attended as a teenager, I had the strange sensation of my genitals burning beneath my dress. For a moment I thought I had an infection, one of those tunnel diseases that is cured only by plungers filled with thick medicine. Then I realized that what I was experiencing was shame. I looked around at the faces of the young people I had grown up with and just knew that they were all imagining me in bed beneath Monty. I realized it was very likely that I was the only member of my old high school crowd who was unmarried and deflowered. It mattered terribly to me.

Throughout my life, I had guarded my virginity unfailingly in the belief that it was the thing that had made me worth marrying. As my church leaders had warned me shrilly, tirelessly against sex, I had thought this was what they were really saying. Now as I anticipated a future without a husband, I couldn't imagine it without a hymen.

II

Perhaps I wouldn't have felt so sullied if I could have escaped the specter of my former sexuality. But when I wasn't confessing to the General Authorities—and I viewed those saintly letters as confessions as guiltily as though they had contained detailed accounts of wild nights—I was still wearing my garments. Once donned, garments are a lifelong commitment, and to leave off wearing them is a terrible sin. So I had to wear them, even when the marriage—the reason I had begun to wear them—had disappeared.

My "garments" changed character remarkably during this time. In marriage, they had been the evidence of my love for God, and despite my great dislike of the aesthetic particulars, the knowledge of them had sometimes suffused me with a sort of confidence as I sat in church surrounded by married women who were also draped in unusual underwear beneath their prim Sunday clothes. It had felt as though we all belonged to the same club.

As a divorcée, I found my friends once again among unmarried women who had never worn garments, and so my own became a memorial to the fact that I didn't belong anywhere. At church socials, these old friends spread out across the chapel lawn in light-colored Bermuda shorts and sleeveless blouses while the hazy Florida sun baked their slender legs and arms. I watched them and thought that they deserved to dress expressively whereas I didn't because I had lost my purity. That is the kind of isolation my garments came to mean. I felt marked instead of graced. One unforgettable night, I learned how deep the isolation ran.

I had begun working as a health-spa attendant at a women's exercise center when I reached Florida. The real fitness craze had not yet overwhelmed America, and there was nothing particularly serious about the spa; it was a roomful of gentle machines that did most of the work, and a very luxurious whirlpool and shower area, where anyone who had broken a sweat against the odds could revive themselves. For a couple of weeks I was a very popular attendant there. I loved the robin's-egg-blue slacks and white shirts I wore every day, loved the pink-and-blue rooms of the club, the thick brilliant carpets, loved talking with people after my months of isolation in Utah. Perhaps in response to my visible pleasure, the women who came to tour the club also loved buying memberships from me.

And then the cleaning service quit. Without warning one day, it was decreed that in the evenings, right before we went home, the attendants would hose out the whirlpool area.

That night the other girls and I lined up on the tile ledge surrounding the whirlpool. The room was dimly lighted and smelled damply of sour disinfectant and sweat. One of the attendants, a girl with black hair to her waist and legs like a Barbie doll's, was shoving hairpins into her ponytail in order to get it off her neck. Then she stepped out of her blue slacks and the other girls all followed suit, tugging at their pants or kicking their way out of them until they were a wall of bare young legs forming a complete ring around me. The girls pulled their shirts over their heads. Wielding spitting hoses, they stood hip to hip in their bras and panties, squealing and with their eyes gleaming, wordlessly ready for the water fight of their lives.

I couldn't see a way out of it. While my co-workers waited, I very slowly pulled my own slacks down to the floor and stood revealed in the baggy, knee-length lower half of my garments. In the back, I could feel them flapping open at the crotch and exposing my buttocks to the fetid air. In the front, they parted so that the other girls could see my pubic hair.

"What are *those*?" somebody asked into a moment of sudden silence.

"They're my underwear," I mumbled, blindly clutching my trousers up around my waist again. Once I had them refastened I stood holding on to the waistband, as though they might slide down of their own accord, maliciously. I broke out of the circle and fled into a dressing booth, where I sat on the narrow bench, my heart pounding. I unhitched my waistband again and slid my hands down into the legs of my pants, one leg at a time, smoothing out my garments where they had rolled and bunched into ridges that I thought were as notice-able as a ball gown would have been beneath my clothes. I stayed there, very still, as the shrill sounds of the water fight gathered force, until the sounds died out altogether and I heard the girls chattering, emptying out of the dressing rooms. Finally the lights went out and yet I continued to sit alone in the dark, too humiliated to move.

My supervisor was working late; I saw a faint light beneath her door as I was leaving at last. I knocked shyly and found her at her neat desk, her head leaning against one hand.

The room was fairly dark, but she and the desk were an island of light beneath a lamp.

"I just needed to tell you that I can't help clean the whirlpool again," I said to her. "I have a religious conflict."

I had been saying this to people all my life. As a kid, I had told my little friends' parents that I couldn't eat in restaurants with them on Sundays because it violated the Sabbath. In a modern-dance class in junior high, I had asked to wear a longer costume than the other dancers, because my father was outraged on religious grounds at the thought of young girls twirling around naked. I had turned down countless cups of coffee and glasses of wine and had never been ashamed of my beliefs, but I was ashamed now. Filled with embarrassment and exhaustion, I stumbled through a fairly uncomplicated version of the story while my boss's startled face clearly communicated her confusion.

"The girls do the cleaning in their underwear, and I wear a form of sacred underwear that no one is supposed to see. I mean, it's a sin for me to let anyone see it," I explained. This part, by the way, was true. "I let everyone see it tonight, because I didn't want you or them to think I was unwilling. But I can't do it again."

The manager's eyes and mouth struggled with disbelief and curiosity and alarm. "Can't you just wear your regular underwear when you clean out the whirlpool?" she finally asked, very kindly.

"This *is* my regular underwear," I said. "This is the underwear I always wear."

Very quickly then, with the air of someone who has decided not to hear any more for her own sake, my supervisor exempted me from whirlpool service. But the harm was already done.

I never went back to the spa again, except to get my check. It wasn't just that I didn't want to face the other girls. It was that I couldn't feel I belonged there with them, since they hadn't yet thrown away their lives.

III

After four or five months in Florida, I moved to Phoenix. The purported reason for relocation—that is, the reason I gave to my parents—was a sudden desire to resume my education that wouldn't be denied. It seemed to make sense to them that the only educational experiences I longed for were those available at Arizona State University in the city adjoining Phoenix that's called Tempe. Perhaps they knew that the real point of my urgency was my need to find somewhere slightly familiar where I was nonetheless completely unknown and would not be compared to the young woman I had been before I'd married. Would not be compared, most particularly, by myself.

In the beginning in Arizona, I reveled in the fact that I attended church every Sunday with a roomful of strangers. The blessed anonymity didn't last, but I didn't mind the change too much at first, because of the source. As soon as my church records arrived for his review, my new bishop, Bishop Mercy, approached me and proposed that we get to know each other. He was very good-looking and young, perhaps thirty-five, and he possessed a powerful, twinkling presence that enabled him to move through the foyer clasping the hands of arriving worshipers as confidently as though they were waters he knew he could part. When he suggested that some

regular counseling sessions were in order because of my suspended temple recommend, I was pleased with the idea. I felt
singled out in a positive way by his interest.

I usually went to his house to consult with him. He and
his sleek red-haired wife and their seven children lived in a
ranch house a half block long that was surrounded by the
quantity of land that attaches itself to the homes of Dallas
socialites. While the Mercy brood made a fearful racket in the
kitchen, the bishop and I sank into deep sofas in the living
room, beneath oil paintings of western vistas and riders on
horseback that my host pointed out to me were originals by
Frederic Remington. I was a little awed by the elegance—not
just the room's elegance, but the bishop's. He dressed at home
in silky pleated trousers and loafers of crushable leather that
were silver-gray and mauve—shoes so exquisite they were almost feminine. I'd never seen anything like either him or his
house.

With a vengeance, he took up in person where my letter-
writing campaign left off, convincing me that my sex life
would remain my church leaders' sole interest in me until I
either remarried or died. Was I dating again? he wanted to
know. Was I dating anyone besides Mormon men? Where did
I allow my beaux to touch me? Nothing more than that? He
didn't say why his interviews were much more frequent and
far-reaching than those of his predecessors, so I assumed he
thought a woman, once awakened, will always remain a hedo-
nist if she isn't watched extremely closely. I didn't suspect that
the presumption of abandon and the priestly prerogative to
ferret out titillating details might have accounted for his great
interest in me. No, I endured his probing in the beginning the
way I had endured the other humiliating events since my
divorce—as though I deserved them. And I might have gone on

that way, completely resigned, until the time when I could finally convince him to restore my temple recommend, except for the fact that after two or three sessions he asked whether I was masturbating.

I didn't feel entirely apprehensive about admitting it; there is so much latitude granted to bishops about the severity with which they *must* denounce sin, and I hoped his attitude toward this matter would be as tolerant as that of my mentor in masturbation, Dr. Johnson. I was still naive enough to expect leniency from a man whose most routine questions were ice picks.

"You've got to stop it. It's a sin," Bishop Mercy said sternly. He wasn't going to give me a break.

I halfheartedly promised him that I wouldn't masturbate anymore. It was such an unimpassioned pledge that when Bishop Mercy called me into his office the next week after Sunday school, I couldn't share with him any reminiscences of a cure. And at that point in my rehabilitation, I didn't yet feel desperate enough to lie.

"This is serious," the bishop scolded me. He appeared to be very out of sorts. "You're going to have to check in with me every week until you quit. I could excommunicate you for this."

It was a possibility so frightening—so unthinkable—that I didn't dare imagine it fully until I was at home alone, surrounded by my plates and my books and the other familiar things that were my anchors. I had always heard excommunication hyped as a blessing by the church authorities who invoked it—a removal of the responsibilities of church membership so that sinners will not continue to defile their covenants and offend God. Still, the few Mormons I'd known who'd been excommunicated had not behaved gratefully. They had either disappeared from church forever or had sat miserably in the congregation while their names were read aloud, staring straight ahead or studying their fingernails. Although usually treated kindly by members-in-good-standing who hoped for their brethren's reform, the outcasts were forbidden to partake of the sacrament or hold church positions during the months and sometimes years that it took to earn back their memberships, and in the meantime they had slunk around the ward house as distrustfully as mistreated dogs.

But if excommunication was unpleasant, it wasn't routine, either, and I knew it couldn't be invoked on a whim. The offenses that merited it were few and, unlike much freewheeling Mormon doctrine, were very specific. Adultery was one of them, but nothing in my memories of youth-night lessons (or my heart) had convinced me so far that the happy orgasms of my private moments were the equivalent of married sex sin. Perhaps Bishop Mercy was wrong?

I was wretched with the knowledge that there was only one person whom I trusted to ask: How I dreaded confessing to my father that I'd become a masturbator of magnitude. On the other hand, I still considered him to be the final authority on church doctrine and everything else.

When I phoned him in Florida, his response was sweeping and serious and enormously calm. He didn't even bother to lecture me, a welcome trend in interaction that was definitely on the rise since my divorce. "You may masturbate twice a day for the rest of your life and no one on earth can threaten your church membership with it," he told me. He added, unnecessarily, "Deborah, I am not actually recommending that you masturbate twice a day."

Although I was relieved by his pronouncement, I wasn't eager to confront Bishop Mercy with my belief that he was wrong. For a while, it seemed easiest just to avoid the man. On Sundays I'd sit on the back row in the chapel and slip out to my car the instant the closing prayer had ended.

But one morning as I was tiptoeing into the church foyer a little late, I saw with dismay that Bishop Mercy hadn't yet abandoned his post as greeter at the main door. He had seen me first and was moving quickly as a quarterback: He intercepted me only a moment later and clasped my shoulders between his hands.

"We need to talk," he said, and he did not release me.

Strangely, I didn't feel paralyzed or afraid. Instead, a movie of unsettling images flickered through my mind: I saw myself sitting in the crook of Monty's arm, awash with a sense of hopelessness; as a desperate seeker in Bishop Rector's office begging to know the secrets of a successful married life; as a listless and ashamed young woman in a hospital bed; as a divorcée barely out of her teens. Seeing myself with such exaggerated clarity, I was suddenly filled with resentment toward the Mormon authority who imprisoned me. I was momentarily such an underdog in my mind's eye that I actually stood up for myself.

Feebly, though. The fear of being eternally misunderstood was infusing me with a paralyzing exhaustion. "I am so tired," I said, more to myself than to Bishop Mercy. "And I don't believe that I've done anything that will allow you to excommunicate me. I really don't."

"I *can* excommunicate you," he said with a slight note of triumph in his voice. He didn't explain. He squeezed my shoulders a last time and released me, then turned on his heel and strode serenely forward, headed for his seat on the podium. I was left behind, dismissed.

Later I came to believe that, deep within himself, he

wasn't necessarily a tyrant. When I soon moved out of his ward and became another bishop's problem, Bishop Mercy didn't track me down and tattle on me to the new man. I was allowed to leave my reputation behind.

IV

My next personal magistrate, Bishop Addlemane, was a much milder person. Despite possessing skin that was the color of oatmeal and a meek personality that matched, Bishop Addlemane was not inclined to roll over and reinstate my temple recommend, either, however. His reasoning had nothing to do with masturbation, a subject that he never inquired into. Bishop Addlemane was simply of the opinion that a lot of time must elapse before I, a divorcée, could be allowed to set foot inside the temple again.

I accepted this attitude, and more interviews, because I'd become desperate. I fiercely wanted my temple recommend back, although not because I yearned for temple worship. Without a recommend, I could never be completely free of Monty. As far as the church was concerned, my civil divorce counted only until death, at which time my temple promises would kick in again and I would become Monty's wife for eternity. I could change my fate only by obtaining a "cancellation of sealing," which is an afterlife divorce. Reinstatement at the temple was the first step in the long journey toward a cancellation of sealing.

My aunt Marie, my father's sister, was the other member of our family who was struggling with the prospect of a complicated eternity. Actually, she was not so much the one struggling as was Uncle Fred, her second husband and partner of thirty years' duration. Aunt Marie had idolized her first husband, Howard, a handsome young pilot who'd died at the end of World War II. She had been "sealed" to Howard during their brief marriage, and she knew that she would live with him in the next life, where church law declared he would also lay claim to the three children whom Uncle Fred had actually sired. It was as though Howard existed in living color, even as a memory, and during all these decades my rather colorless uncle Fred had just been filling in for him so that Howard wouldn't lose his place.

I had always regarded the convolutions of Aunt Marie's married life as something of a joke. This was not because its circumstances seemed ridiculous—I accepted as normal the intricacies of Mormon marriage—but because I couldn't suppress hilarious imaginings when I contemplated the reunion ahead. People who'd known her as a bride said Marie had been a lovely girl, with shining eyes and a real fashion sense, but I knew her only as an uninquisitive woman of magnificently increasing size, with a shrill nature that made allowances for no one. I couldn't believe that the glamorous dead husband my aunt Marie still adored would want to spend eternity with her.

Now, all at once, Howard's dilemma didn't seem very funny to me. I was suddenly too aware that temple "sealings" not only join you to another forever, but hog-tie you there—that I, too, might spend eternity with someone I didn't love.

By the time I fell into the hands of Bishop Addlemane, my desire to put Monty behind me completely had become a focus for my life. I was dating again, not seriously but with an increasing feeling that I had very little to offer the young men who interested me. Not only had I already surrendered my virtue but I wasn't really free, in that no church leader had been able to assure me that I wouldn't be forced to spend the afterlife locked into a marriage I didn't want. I could not guarantee eternity to my suitors, and eternity mattered to them, and to me—it was far more important than the eighty years or so on earth that came before it, and more real. I was looking for loopholes.

V

I inhabited a no-man's-land as a divorcée, but it wasn't defined only by humiliation. As I struggled to get through a situation I'd never imagined, I was sometimes surprised by flickering moments of freedom that I couldn't fully enjoy, since I didn't know release was the thing I was feeling.

I had acquired a roommate, Madeline, a friend who attended a student ward at ASU with me. The ward became the center of our social lives and Madeline found a boyfriend there, a witty and brawny young man named Daniel. At least she claimed Daniel was her boyfriend long before I saw any evidence of alliance. For months the three of us spent most of our leisure time togther, as though we were an unbreakable set. Very little that was exclusive seemed to be going on between my friends.

When their status changed, it was dramatically. I came home from a late class one evening and found that the door to the bedroom Madeline and I shared was pointedly closed; from behind it were coming unmistakable yips and giggles. Madeline and Daniel never appeared for dinner, never even poked their heads out into the living room to ask whether I minded the way the bedroom had been commandeered. At bedtime, I stepped out of my dress and lay down on the sofa in my garments, wrapped up in a sheet I'd retrieved from the linen closet. I could hear Madeline actually cry out occasionally. I admit that I strained to hear.

The experience was an entirely new one for me, given the ironclad chastity that was preached at BYU and that the kids I knew had practiced. I felt some embarrassment about being so close to sex, certainly—what else could explain the way I had just been creeping around in the kitchen, trying not to crack plates together or slam cupboard doors, as though I didn't want to interrupt a church service? But primarily I was hugely relieved. In recent months, so much attention had been focused upon my own sexuality that I had begun to feel like the only woman in the world who yearned for orgasm. Some part of me had begun to believe that, even in my sexually inactive state, my desires defined me as terribly weak and prone to sin. As I eavesdropped enthusiastically on Madeline's warblings, I knew at last that, even if I was depraved, I wasn't alone. It was a tremendous unburdening.

In the morning over breakfast, we all treated each other with the elaborate politeness we'd have adopted if we'd just had an argument. After that we were never a threesome again but the awkwardness ceased. Whenever Daniel stayed over, he and Madeline used the couch. Each time they used it, my relief increased and my surprise at myself deepened.

I certainly believed on some level that I should denounce the celebratory sex going on in the next room with a regularity that I frankly envied, but I never could work myself up to it. In fact, I actually enjoyed the atmosphere of sex that now enshrouded our apartment—loved the way Daniel casually squeezed a buttock or a breast when he and Madeline watched television together, loved walking past them in the early morning while they slept, naked and tightly entwined and barely covered with a sheet. Loved particularly the moans of pleasure that traveled more and more freely through the walls as my friends quit restraining themselves. I sometimes waited for them to climax the way generations of Americans have been able to fall asleep only above the patter of Johnny Carson.

I welcomed their open eroticism not only because I was less ashamed of myself in its presence, but because their lovemaking was voluntary and joyful. My own experiences hadn't exposed me to such lovemaking, but now I could at least imagine it. I think I may have enjoyed their affair nearly as much as they did, because of all it portended for me. On some level, and for just a while, I felt rescued from a passionless future.

But my vicarious pleasure didn't last long. When Madeline became pregnant, everyone's joy drained immediately out of the house. She was twenty-five years old and eager to marry, but Daniel was only nineteen and still playing with the idea that he'd go on a mission. Their breakup was inevitable and underscored by the recriminations Madeline shouted into the phone once Daniel was no longer coming over.

She moved back to her mother's in Phoenix, and right before her baby, Geoffrey, was born I dropped in to see her. If I'd maintained any personal wonder over the ecstatic nature of her early affair, I lost it then. Within minutes I was transported back to where I'd started before I knew her, trussed up tightly with wide bands of resentment and near-despair.

Madeline was in the den of her mother's comfortable house, her swollen feet propped up on a coffee table and her hands resting on her enormous stomach. She had become diabetic in the last stages of pregnancy, so she wasn't feeling well—but she also wasn't feeling at all shunned or wounded, which was the condition I'd expected from a Mormon unwed mother. She couldn't say enough about the way her ward members were rallying to support her emotionally, or about her generous bishop, who was always phoning to see what sort of financial help she needed or whether she'd like to borrow his wife's own bassinette. She said that her baby was going to have five hundred different parents, all of them ward members with an abiding interest in the baby's mother.

"Hasn't anyone, well, said anything rude to you?" I couldn't help finally blurting. "Hasn't your bishop at least asked you to repent?"

She appeared to be genuinely surprised by the question. "Why, no," she said. "Everyone just talks about the baby. Everyone is *excited* about the baby."

Certainly there is great reverence among Mormons for motherhood, an oft-stated belief that it's a woman's highest purpose. Maybe Madeline's impending motherhood made her acceptable somehow, in spite of the way she'd achieved it. Or maybe it was just that she was in a difficult position, and people love to prop up someone who needs them. Perhaps she was simply blessed with a home ward of kindly and liberal thinkers. Whatever the case, as I drove away from her house that night I was raging inwardly that Madeline was being celebrated for her condition at the same time that I was being suspected and condemned for mine, which wasn't nearly so saturated with sin.

At my next appointment with Bishop Addlemane, my confusion and belligerence were very fresh. "I want to know why you're treating me like a fallen woman," I demanded. "I want to know why you're denying me a temple recommend and a cancellation of sealing when I haven't done anything wrong. I want to know why I have to write all these letters and why you continue to cross-examine me when the entire history of my sex life consists of sleeping with my husband, while he was my husband."

I had hoped for discombobulation, but none of my new aggressiveness threw him. With a complacency that I had begun to recognize among the men consulting on my future, he said that everything I objected to had occurred only for my protection. He said that the promises I had made to God in the temple—one of which had concerned sexual fidelity—were such important ones, and the repercussions for violating them were so severe, that they warranted monitoring.

Once again I felt thick exhaustion pooling in my veins as I realized Bishop Addlemane was unable to understand my anger. I was completely cornered. I had no idea how to retain my dignity during this process of "forgiveness" I'd become involved in, or how to end it.

VI

I guess that Bishop Addlemane saw my discouragement and made a concession. He set up an interview for me with his superior in the church, a "stake president" by the name of Randall Wainwright. ("Stakes" are geographical regions made up of a number of "wards.") He said that if President Wainwright decided that I had proved myself worthy, his opinion could be a very influential one with the Salt Lake leaders who stood to end the embargo on my temple recommend.

I willed myself to numbness before I drove over to President Wainwright's the next evening. I thought it would be easier to get through another of these talks if I refused to consider very deeply anything that was said. Pulling up in front of the correct house, I paid deliberate attention to visual things, as though that would keep my awarenesses from going farther. I saw the building's bright white paint, the brown stubble of winter lawn, the absence of shrubbery that made the house look abandoned.

The door was answered by a short, extremely wide woman with frowsy hair who was wearing a purple muumuu. This was Mrs. Wainwright. She ushered me into the small bedroom that doubled as her husband's study, and President Wainwright rose from behind his Formica desk. He was a fabulously tall man in his sixties with hands the size of kitchen mitts. His face was rather kind.

He questioned me for about an hour, but his questions came so slowly that I could never hold on to a train of thought and figure out where he was headed. He inquired how long I had known Monty before I married him—it startled me, because no one else had ever asked—and posed a variety of questions about "moral cleanliness." He waited for every answer with an identical expression of slightly vacant interest and nodded rhythmically whenever I was speaking without appearing to actually hear me.

At one point he adopted an expression of unusually deep reflection. Another of the interminable pauses fell, such a long one that I thought the interview might be over, that he had reached whatever conclusion he was going for. He began to speak, as though to share his conclusion.

He asked, "Did your husband ever *mouth* you?"

I am nearly forty now, and I have seen something of the world, and I have discussed sex with friends and strangers, sometimes in bars, where propriety gets suspended. But the only person who has asked me whether I've ever had oral sex is President Wainwright, who I believe is also the only person who has wanted to know.

"No," I said. It wasn't the truth, but I was no longer the girl who, just two years earlier, had nearly wept at the realization that she had lied to a church leader.

President Wainwright shook his head sorrowfully. "I haven't ever mouthed my wife, either," he said.

This, as it turned out, was the final thought that passed between us. President Wainwright never said anything about the question of my temple recommend, which may not have interested him.

VII

I never wondered about the shape of Monty's life, didn't need to know whether he was challenged or loved. When we were first apart I did assume, however, that he was also tooling over to his bishop's place with terrible frequency to confess every moment when his hands cupped a new woman's breasts, or wanted to. I assumed that our temple recommends would be withheld for the same period of time, and that when we became eligible again, he would be as anxious to proceed with a "cancellation of sealing" as I.

Instead, after only a year, I heard through friends that he had remarried in the temple. It had not been a problem for him to reclaim his recommend, and it had not been required, as it was required for me, for our "sealing" to be canceled in order for him to forge another. When the United States government outlawed polygamy in the 1800s, Mormon men had caved in only temporarily and reluctantly, and they still plotted through a rarely mentioned maneuver to practice plural marriage later. Although a man might be separated from his wives in this life by death and divorce, he was actually laying up for himself treasure in heaven: There was no limit to the number of wives he could retain for the next life, whereas a woman was limited to one partner.

More than six months after my interview with President Wainwright, my bishop finally phoned me without warning to say my temple recommend had been reinstated by the Salt Lake City authorities. When I asked him about the procedure for applying for a "cancellation of sealing," he said that it wasn't time to consider taking that step. I was never to meet a bishop who thought it was time.

Bishop Addlemane had phoned me in the morning. Afterward, I went back to bed and slept straight through until nightfall, something I hadn't done since Monty and I were still together and the days were too long to bear.

Seven

I

When I remarried it was automatically, the way I wash my hands after handling the dog. I was ridding myself of the stain of divorce as best I could. Discouraged that my cancellation of sealing was stalemated, I became vulnerable to an offer that a year or two before I might not have considered—an offer from a Gentile.

I met Lowell during a game of water volleyball at the singles apartment complex in Phoenix where we both lived. I was wearing a pink bikini and he was a lot thinner then. I was drawn to his rubbery face that emitted a constant stream of one-liners and to his extravagant head of utterly black, utterly straight hair. Most of all, I couldn't resist his fabulous tallness, a height so extreme that I came barely past his shoulder and knew at last what it was to feel dainty.

On the surface, I didn't consider it a serious romance. As I tried to finish college in the wake of Madeline's departure, I was living with a group of Mormon schoolteachers, all of them lively, pretty, devout young women who wouldn't have dreamed of dating a non-Mormon. Because I courted their approval of me, I pretended to them for a while that the friendship with Lowell, a divorced mechanical engineer who did not even believe in God, was casual. I even pretended to myself that nothing could come of a relationship with a man who did not share my beliefs, who was twenty years my senior, whose first marriage had been disquieting, and who was very recently and grudgingly divorced. I said to myself that the thought of Lowell as marriage material was absurd.

In truth, however, our relationship was quickly, completely, intense and careening toward the altar. From my end, it took this form because—whatever I told myself—I didn't have the slightest idea how to relate to any man except as marriage material, and because I wanted terribly to belong to someone. Since I was damaged goods, some part of me was now willing to settle into a respectable life with someone who wanted me but wasn't a Mormon, and then try to bring him into the fold.

And Lowell certainly wanted me as no other man ever had, wanted me in a way that consumed him. It showed in his near-desperate need for time with me that made him testy when I needed to study or wanted to go to dinner with my girlfriends. It showed in the way he quickly arranged to introduce me to his four near-grown children, his powerful hand gripping my waist and pulling me in closely against him, as though to merge us physically in front of the people who were at the center of his world.

Our discussions of marriage were held early in the enormous four-poster that I was always amazed Lowell had managed to wedge through the door to his apartment. We spent a lot of time in this bed because I enjoyed his hands upon me. The narrow range of our activities within it would probably have surprised many of Lowell's cronies, however, some of whom were fresh from their own divorces in the 1970s and were discovering the age of sexual liberation. I know that it certainly surprised me that an experienced man was willing to settle for what little satisfaction I offered him.

At first, feeling mindful of the letters I was still sending off to Salt Lake City, I would allow Lowell only to lie alongside me and chastely hold me. In time, I agreed that his hands should wander slightly, although never below the waist. I was gratified by his great love, which apparently made it possible for him to honor my prim standards without complaint.

As our courtship deepened, the amount of self-control that Lowell needed steadily increased. I felt daring and uneasy about our overnight trysts, but they were cruelly disappointing for Lowell, principally because of the nightgown I always wore, which was a forbidding one. It was floor-length and made of thick yellow flannel, with a turtleneck and cuffs so elasticized they were viselike. The area from breast to crotch was appliquéd with a huge red apple that I often saw Lowell eyeing with a clear distaste for my delight in symbolism. Holding on to me in this thing as I tossed and turned in my sleep was probably as arousing as clutching a bale of cotton. And of course, he also had to contend with my garments, about which he tried to be polite while always subtly working for change. He was very skilled at this: He was able, with a few words and a sigh on occasion, to help me perceive my garments through new eyes.

"Do you think you'll always wear them?" he asked me once, wistfully, his hand beneath my blouse but still unable to reach my breasts because of all the nylon. And another time: "You know, they're just *clothes*."

These small remarks, made at the right time, took root in a powerful way. I had never thought before that I might *not* always wear them. I had never considered that they could be anything less than a sacred trust. But Lowell's hints created a crack in my ethical armor that desire was able to pierce through, and the desire was fierce. In time I yearned so deeply to remove my garments that I became capable of unimaginable things.

In the beginning, I took them off only when I slept at Lowell's place, slipping out of them when I changed into my nightgown and leaving them folded and carefully covered with a towel in the bathroom. At first I kept rousing from sleep and thinking guiltily of my garments lying only a few yards away; I hoped they would continue to protect me from harm, since they were still practically in the room. A few times my guilt won out, and I padded into the bathroom for my underwear so that the last hours before dawn could be untroubled. One night I retrieved my garments during an electrical storm because I was afraid I'd be struck by lightning if I wasn't wearing them.

Pretty soon, however, I could sleep through the night without them, and so I left my garments behind once during the day as well. I remember how wide my freed legs seemed to swing as I loped across campus to class, remember the dig from the elastic on the panties I'd just bought that weren't the right size. As I sat through a lecture surrounded by young women wearing underwear just like mine, I was one of them at last. After that, sin was more of a cinch.

I wore my garments less and less and shopped more and more for revealing clothes. I was overwhelmed with the pleasure of reclaiming my youth, but still I always returned to my garments eventually. They were a little more dear to me now that I wasn't always wearing them, the way a cloying lover's value is enhanced once he stops insisting that you stay close at hand. And I also cherished them out of fear—the fear of being forsaken by God if I stopped wearing the things altogether. I knew I was tiptoeing up to that dangerous line and sometimes I was terrified. It's a very serious thing to stop wearing garments; for me, it was far more serious than even divorce had been. The regulations of the garments had been very strictly adhered to in my family, plus they were bound up in my mind with the menacing pledges that had to do with disemboweling and throat slitting that had been extracted from me in the temple. At the worst, I thought that I might be killed—by what? by whom?—if I discarded them. At the least, I thought I'd be left unprotected in the world—that I'd be performing the equivalent of throwing away a magic shield.

By the time Lowell and I got engaged, I had finally hit upon a rationalization that allowed me to take the momentous step, seeing as how it seemed to relate to God's own social priorities. I told myself that Lowell, whether he was a Mormon or not, was the heir to the patriarchal order and would be the head of our house. I told myself that I should submit to him as my husband, even in matters of raiment.

I was very frightened on the day I finally relegated my garments to the past in a ceremony of prayer and voodoo that I hoped would appease any heavenly onlookers. I had by then a couple of dozen pairs, many of them rubbed to silky transparency in places where the slight nap of the nylon-blend fabric had worn away. Depending on their age, they ranged from stark white to discolored yellow. I gathered them into a soft pile and carried them out onto the little concrete porch that adjoined my apartment. I mounded them together on the concrete and crouched down beside them, clutching a pair of scissors and a book of matches.

I snipped the temple markings—the sacred portions of the garments—out of each pair, leaving holes in the fabric that could have been the work of killer moths. Divested of their markings, the clothes themselves were secular and meaningless. I had even seen my parents toss their worn-out, newly ventilated garments in among the household rags, piquing the curiosity of the succession of maids who used them on the furniture.

According to the teachings of the church, I had to dispose properly of the markings, although I couldn't remember whether a method had ever been specified. I improvised by setting the markings on fire, and as the embers died out I prayed over them. "Dear Heavenly Father, I hope You understand that I haven't turned my back on everything between us just because I'm not going to wear these anymore," I said to Him. "I hope this act won't blind You to the faithful things I still do."

My heart was pounding. I swept the ashes into my hands and walked to the edge of the porch so I could spread them in the grass.

It was over, and I was more elated than I could have imagined. My heart and loins pulsed with a thrill of danger that was almost sexual, but I also felt utterly helpless and unprotected, as though I were a soft, stripped sapling an inch thick that could be snapped in two by someone's hands. That sensation of vulnerability would last for years.

When Lowell took me to dinner that night, I kept feeling my small breasts swing directly into my brassiere. I confused the titillation with an affection for Lowell: I was filled with surprise and wonder all the way through dessert.

II

I was a very pliable girl, and I hated hurting anyone's feelings. This is part of the reason that I married two men in a row without really wanting to. The other part, of course, was that I didn't know another way to live; nothing in my Mormon upbringing had suggested that other satisfactions might bring me happiness. And thus I soon became Mrs. Lowell Bateman.

I didn't understand why I didn't love Lowell, because I was fairly attracted to him and knew that he possessed lovable qualities: He was very intelligent and he told interesting stories about his years in graduate school, which he'd spent in Germany studying under a brilliant mentor. I had always valued the ability to tell stories beyond nearly everything else in my close companions.

Certainly, he loved me with a devotion that never abated and that expressed itself in silk scarves that appeared unbidden in my dresser drawers and record albums that I would mention wanting and then hear blaring out of the stereo. He listened to me tirelessly, and unlike Monty, he didn't have a laundry list of precisely acceptable behaviors that he thought I should conform to.

But he was also a desperately lonely man, and the cave of his inner emptiness was one that I instinctively didn't want to live in. Both his parents had died during Lowell's early childhood, and afterward, he and his two small sisters were parceled out to different homes and lost to one another forever. His first wife, a sculptor, had buried herself in her art until she had barely minded—or noticed—their divorce. As a result of abandonments, his soul was poisoned: A profound well of alienation and distrust lay just beneath the surface of his humorous agreeability.

Many was the night when he didn't come to bed and I would pad upstairs to find him drinking alone in his den, his face a study in vague and persecuted grief. When an expected promotion didn't materialize toward the end of our first year together, he confronted his supervisor, according to the version of the story he told me, not out of a wellspring of righteous indignation, as though he'd been unjustly passed over and wanted to know why, but out of paranoia, as though he were accustomed to being senselessly denied. Without understanding it fully, I knew that his need for me to commit to him completely was too great for me to fulfill.

Still, divorce had taught me things I didn't want to know about ruination and loneliness, and I certainly appreciated my new sense of wifehood and belonging. Except for his kids, Lowell was unfettered by close relatives or obligations and was completely free to become my family. He spent more time with me, puttering and playing, than anyone ever has again. So, on the whole, the marriage didn't fill me with despair, at least not in the beginning.

Lowell bought us a big, unmodern house in Tempe, near the university so that I could continue with classes there. Most of the big rooms were painted a faded yellow that imbued them with a blankness that was practically institutional. We didn't repaint for the longest time, and it was like living in a hospital. Whatever the house's shortcomings, however, the carpets were so luxurious that we rarely wore shoes, and I had a tiny study of my own that received constant sun and that opened into the rest of the house through French doors.

The house sat on a vast lot that was dense with citrus trees, and Lowell proved to be expert at cultivating a garden. During my years with him, under the expert tutelage of the other wives in the Relief Society, I learned to put up our plump tomatoes in bottles and to brew caldrons of thick marmalade, then line the shelves in the storeroom with the colorful fruits of my labors. Sometimes I stood back and examined the rows and rows of vegetables and jams in their neatly labeled jars and felt for the first time like a truly accomplished person, so adept was I becoming at the activities of canning and preserving that are a measure of mastery among Mormon women.

III

As automatically as I had married, I began seeing Michael Clark again.

He was an old boyfriend, someone I had been dating when I met Lowell. A Mormon man, tall and heavy, with eyebrows like bottle brushes and a tendency to perspire that left his shirts always stained beneath his arms. There had been something faintly distasteful in his kiss that had to do with the rubbery texture of his lips. On a romantic level, he had never appealed to me at all.

But if he hadn't made my heart sing, he had fascinated me. He was the first religious man I'd known who would outright question the views of the General Authorities, and who liked disrespectful, funny women instead of meek home-makers. In fact, far from being alarmed by my divorce or my agitation with the church authorities who were making me miserable in the months following it, my angry response to life's complications seemed only to reassure him that I was spirited.

We did not have an elegant dating history. Michael was a designer of washing-machine parts, whose career was embryonic. He had rented a dusty office in an old building and filled it with odds and ends of wire and metal pieces heaped together in shallow cartons, stuck at random onto open shelves. We spent a great deal of time together there while he crouched on the floor, tinkering with pliers and configurations of what appeared to be flotsam. He worked in an absentminded way, keeping up a rambling critical commentary about the music blaring out of the stereo or whatever problem of the universe he and I were working out together. Usually he went home early.

Although I experienced a sweet flow of friendship during these unfrantic afternoons, I wasn't confident about Michael's future and I never took him seriously as a suitor. So I was surprised that when I told him about Lowell, his body became so immediately charged that it seemed to have gotten larger. "I don't think this will make you happy in the long run," he said, his voice filling with conviction. "I don't think you're going to be satisfied, trying to make a life outside the church with a man."

I was annoyed by his advice, but Michael persisted. "I think you should give our relationship more of a chance. Promise me you'll pray about it," he said. He declared that he wanted to marry me.

I promised, but I didn't pray; my faith in divine revelations about marriage had not survived my divorce. Besides, for the first time, my belief that I should marry any good Mormon who asked me was weaker than my distaste for marrying the man who had asked.

When he returned a few days later, I was sitting in my bedroom. Its window afforded a view of the front door, and on the closed drapes I could see his shadow, the dark arc of his arm as he raised it to knock. "Deborah!" he called, several times. I'm sure he knew I was inside, but I didn't answer. I didn't see him again until Lowell and I had been married for more than a year.

By then I was living the very turmoil Michael had prophesied for me, and so I came to him—like all infidels—searching for the thing I was missing: in this case, some time with a man with a religious heart who shared my beliefs. I told myself, and him, that I wanted only that, but it quickly got away from me.

The fact that I was married to a non-Mormon hadn't been too difficult in the beginning. But as the months passed, I minded being the only married woman in the ward without a husband who attended services. More important, I was stung by the constant reminders that my household was impotent, since the priesthood wields the power of God in Mormondom. When the bishop sermonized in church about the importance of fathers gathering their families together for communal prayer, I sat and watched my folded hands. When one of the other wives in Relief Society said that her husband had given a priesthood blessing to their sick daughter, and had cured her, I could suddenly feel the pulse in my throat. When the "home teachers" dropped by our house once a month—they were men from the ward, and it was their priesthood assignment to visit Lowell and me and other families, to see if we needed any assistance—I sat wracked with embarrassment. Is everything going well in your marriage? they wanted to know. Are you having any financial problems? Any spiritual ones? While Lowell resisted their well-meaning questions with a silent hostility that communicated his belief they were prying, I began to yearn for a husband who understood what God expected from a man.

If I had married him feeling that no deserving Mormon man should be saddled with me, I hadn't considered how it would wear on me to live with someone who wasn't a deserving Mormon man. At some point, even Michael began to look very good. The first time Michael took me in his arms, I even thought the embrace might be justified, that God might understand my disloyalty since it was being enacted in His name.

Once we came together again, Michael and I were very careful never to have sex. Our most torrid times were a few afternoons when I lay down on his office sofa and Michael crouched over me for a few minutes, covering my face and neck with wet kisses and cupping my breasts beneath my blouse in his thick-fingered hands. How delectable those kisses were; I felt their flavor invade my mouth and creep all the way down my throat, to my heart. Michael was no longer the overweight, disheveled man I had once tried not to kiss. Now he was a man of God.

As long as our genitalia did not touch, I was able to believe I was upholding the church's "moral" standards. I knew that "morality" referred only to intercourse and that, without it, no cheating had occurred. This belief was not unique to me. Every weekend, sweethearts living in Salt Lake City, in the shadow of the temple, writhed naked together in front of their fireplaces, their hands or their tongues bringing each other again and again to orgasm. And when they finished, they buttoned themselves calmly back into their clothes and kissed at the door, secure in the thought that they had once again upheld God's commandments. That is the way the questions of good and evil can become hairsplittingly resolved among people to whom everything that is free-flowing and human is forbidden. And that is how Michael and I justified ourselves.

Our trysts would end when I returned home to prepare dinner for my husband. I cut onions into tiny cubes, browned fragrant hamburger, filled a waiting casserole dish with fat blanched noodles and thinned soup from a can. I watched my hands as I worked—young, pretty hands that already were gnarling a little with arthritis, so that the knuckles seemed to express a strength of character I didn't think to analyze whether I possessed. I liked the look of my hands and liked being there in the kitchen. Night after night, I was the perfect wife.

IV

I don't know how Lowell discovered my betrayal, but his response was terrifying. I came home one day to find that his face was made of wax and was melting into a ghastly distortion of itself—the nose too long, the lips suddenly too stringy, the cheeks pulled down into a grimace that ended on his throat. When I came in he was standing in the hallway next to the kitchen, writing all over the yellow walls with a blue Magic Marker. His little-boy script had gone completely wild; it exploded out at senseless angles and his letters were a dozen different sizes as he wrote, over and over, "Deborah loves Michael, Deborah loves Michael."

He wasn't violent, but I think he really went insane for a while. He was in more pain than he could bear. One moment his kiss against my neck would be as pleading as a child's, and in the next he would be standing over me while I tried to sleep, his voice a siren: "I married you because I thought you were a religious girl! I thought you were different! I thought you would be faithful!"

He had been patient with my chastity during our courtship not for the reason I'd assumed—out of respect for my beliefs—but because my primness had reassured him. He had thought me a woman whose convictions would guarantee companionship. He had thought I could make up to him for the hurts in his past.

The force of Lowell's grief overcame us both very quickly. When he wasn't berating or begging me, he was drinking. When I wasn't stonewalling him or bawling, I retreated to the corner of our L-shaped couch. I huddled there for the length of nearly every day, crocheting an afghan in long rows of red, white, and blue. I was very nimble with a crochet hook then. I crocheted through Lowell's ravings and through his words of love and sometimes I crocheted through the night. I thought crocheting might hold me together while Lowell came apart.

It proved to be a fragile defense, however, and I soon succumbed to a depression like the one that had swallowed me as I'd steeled myself to end my first marriage. This one was deeper, however. I had so much more for which to loathe myself.

The phenomenon of emotional battering has become a more widely recognized one in the years since all this occurred, so that even isolated women who keep in touch only through TV and the newsmagazines may have some chance of knowing when it happens to them. I didn't have that advantage in 1976. In the absence of information and in the warp of space and time that occurred around Lowell's rage, I soon could barely force my eyes open in the mornings. I was leaden with shame.

I began to experience a powerful love for him, in the way that I now know you can come to love a jailer. I wrote him a string of letters even though we were in the same house. I wrote after he was asleep, on blue onionskin, and left the letters on his desk so he would find them in the morning. Over and over, I chastised myself and congratulated him for his love for me, and his kindness.

When I had any energy, I'd undertake a project intended to please him. He was fixated on a pair of skimpy white shorts he believed that I'd worn often around Michael, so one afternoon I cut them into small pieces and drove the shreds to a Dumpster. I told him about it when he came home, told him as radiantly as though I were giving him an affectionate gift.

I knew at times that I was becoming very bizarre, and even Lowell didn't oppose my wish to see a therapist. I found a Dr. Pointer, another Mormon doctor who, like his predecessor, Dr. Johnson, primarily regaled me with stories about Mormon couples who were more happily (and more conventionally) married than I. Dr. Pointer was not without compassion, though: He suggested rather kindly that I needed time out from trauma and wondered whether I'd like to enter a hospital. As soon as he brought it up, I could hardly wait to go.

Although I was delighted to be sleeping away from Lowell, I soon discovered myself to be sleeping in an unenlightened psychiatric facility instead, primarily a holding tank for middle-aged, depressed housewives. A couple of times a day one of the patients would shuffle into a narrow room at the end of the hall, always accompanied by the same dignified, grandfatherly psychiatrist who presided there. When the gray-green door swung open with the comings and goings of the nurses, I thought I could see that my compatriots were strapped to a table and that something resembling electrodes was stuck to their skulls. Above the waiting, deadened faces of these women the headgear took on the appearance of curlers. In that unmoving hospital, even the violence of shock treatments got blurred until it was unalarming.

Spared such treatments, I stayed groggy on antidepressants and roused myself only for sessions with Dr. Pointer or visits from Lowell. Mainly I waited listlessly to go home, not wanting to and not knowing exactly what improvement the doctor was watching for that would convince him I was ready. Nothing occurred that could be called an event until finally I created one by phoning Michael.

I hadn't seen Michael since Lowell's discovery of our "affair," but the phone call wasn't about passion. I simply knew that he would come if I asked and that he would be kind to me, as he always had been. I knew that everything about him would be predictable, where nothing else had made sense to me for weeks.

I was sitting outside the door to my room, still working on the afghan I'd brought from home, when I realized that my friend was standing over me. The afghan was very large by then; it flowed out of my chair and surrounded it with voluminous folds. When I looked up into Michael's face, I was unnerved enough that I gathered the whole blanket into my lap and began clutching it and plucking at it nervously, until he leaned over and steadied my hands by holding them in both of his.

We were never alone during his visit, but I was able to ask him the question I had been longing to pose to someone who wouldn't punish me with the answer: Did it mean I was crazy that I had come to this hospital?

"I don't know very much about these things, but I can tell just from looking at you that you're not crazy," he said to me. "And whatever the reason you're here, it doesn't scare me. It doesn't make me want to be with you any less." My whole body relaxed a little bit after his reassurances.

If the nurses on my ward didn't provide much in the way of rehabilitation, they were truly first-rate at spying and reporting. Before Lowell came into my room the next day he knew all about my visitor. He raged and he reproached me and he finally left. I stood in front of my dim mirror. My hair was lank against my neck and my eyes were so swollen and red that they resembled lips. I stared at myself and wondered what it was that Lowell and Michael didn't want to live without.

V

The next night when Lowell arrived, he ushered me into a large, frigid room down the hall from mine where the walls were painted khaki. On all of the walls, bulletin boards covered with cork obscured the dull-colored paint in patches; the boards had been punctured with so many tacks that the surfaces were pitted and picked away. The other furnishings were primarily metal folding chairs lined up in a couple of half-hearted rows or collapsed and stacked against the walls, plus a few wooden armchairs pushed off to the side. It was a lecture hall, as glaringly lighted from overhead as an operating room.

Standing in a disorderly semicircle inside the door were my bishop and his two assistants, all of them flashing the sorts of unthinking grins that accompany the hearty handshakes of strangers. They were middle-aged men of three different sizes—short, medium, tall—and they were all wearing similar gray suits and shiny, round-toed brown shoes. Unrestrained air-conditioning was blasting out of a hole in the ceiling where an acoustical tile was missing, and the force of the airstream was standing the men's hair on end, as though from static electricity. I was very surprised to see them.

"We're here to find out whether anything has gone on that would warrant an excommunication court, Sister Bateman," my bishop, John Lawton, said to me, his fervent smile never faltering.

We seated ourselves in the armchairs, which appeared ready to splay apart. The foam cushions had once been upholstered with wide stripes in orange and brown, but now the fabric had split and practically worn away. When I stood up again, crumbs of foam rubber would cling to the seat of my napped bathrobe. The appearance of this would seem strangely in keeping with the dishevelment of the robe, which I had been wearing every day for two weeks.

The three men sat in a straight line directly across from Lowell and me. Lowell had pulled our two chairs very close together, as though in alliance.

"It was important to your husband that you answer our questions," John Lawton continued, still beaming. "He has brought this matter to us because it is one that falls within our jurisdiction, as your ward leaders."

Lowell was holding my hand throughout this slight

speech. I wasn't sure I wanted him to hold it, so my hand kept clenching into a little ball within his, then relaxing slightly. I never actually pulled away, because I didn't want him to begin doubting again that I wanted to remain his wife.

"We need to ask you about your relationship with Michael Clark," John Lawton was saying, still with that jarring cordiality. "We need to know what went on." I began fidgeting as I watched his unrestrainedly smiling face, certain that there was something terribly wrong in the way the men who had come to determine my future were perceiving the fissure in my marriage.

I tried to tell the story of my friendship with Michael as coherently as I could. At first I was embarrassed to confess, but then confession began rolling out of me with a furious, healing energy. "We snuck around to see each other for a long time," I told the bishop. I rushed to cleanse my soul.

John Lawton's eyes stopped me; nothing within them was flickering. It was as though my words weren't registering, as though he were seated across from me in a soundproof booth, smiling through the glass. His constant smile began to seem actually menacing.

When my discourse about disloyalty ran down, John asked his question. "Was there any actual sexual intercourse?" he wanted to know.

"There was only some kissing," I said.

He nodded and smiled. "And are you willing to discontinue this relationship?"

"I've already told Lowell that I will."

He smiled and nodded, and rose. His silent advisers rose with him, and they all came toward us. Lowell and I also got out of our chairs automatically, and the bishop and his counselors clasped our hands in turn, as though they were making the rounds to congratulate us. I was feeling horribly confused.

"There were some unwise decisions made, but I don't see that there has been any wrongdoing that would warrant an excommunication court," John Lawton was saying. I didn't know what he meant for a minute, and then I realized that I could only be excommunicated if I had actually slept with Michael. All the rest of it—the betrayal of Lowell's emotions, the fact that our homelife had deteriorated at my hands to the point where I'd retreated to a mental institution to avoid it—were not excommunicable offenses, and were being ignored. As I had known while seeing Michael, only sex was a sin.

"This will all blow over," John Lawton was saying to me, and he patted my shoulder fondly, although I had been attending his ward for only a year and didn't know him very well. "You two just be good to each other."

I was afraid to look at Lowell directly when this was said. As we had faced Lawton together, my hand so deeply anchored within Lowell's that I had felt imprisoned, I had finally figured out his motives through the medicated haze that was slowing down all my perceptions. It seemed to me that when he had discovered I couldn't respect him without the priesthood, he had insisted on calling me to account for hurting him in front of the men I did respect. He was filled with the need for vindication. I feared how it would affect him that he wasn't getting any.

He and I accompanied my church leaders all the way down the hall to the entrance to the hospital ward. They chatted with us along the way, but they never commented upon where they were. They didn't seem to notice the spiritless patients slumped in their bathrobes in the chairs that lined the walls, or that I was one of them.

VI

John Lawton lived at the end of our street. His house was the chaotic one in the cul-de-sac, where the lawn was filled with paint-splattered workmen and the skeleton of a sprawling addition was slowly filling out the side yard.

When I sat on our front patio at a certain angle, I could see most of the Lawton house. I watched it often when I first came home from the hospital and was still feeling too scattered to do anything else. I saw trucks pull up with their loads of dry wall, and sometimes I saw John Lawton's plump wife, Loretta, arrive in her long car that was always filled with children, some of whom belonged to her and others who lived in the neighborhood. As Loretta and the kids streamed past the workmen and in through the front door, nearly all of the house that I could see disappeared behind a blur of humans.

One evening when John pulled into his driveway after work, he noticed that I was sitting alone. It wasn't dark yet, wasn't quite dinnertime, so he strolled over to visit with me. He pulled his lawn chair very close to mine and I remember that he smelled strongly of soap, as though he'd thoroughly scrubbed his hands before leaving the insurance office where he worked downtown.

Behind us, I could feel my own house pressing in on my back. Lowell and I had painted the wall next to the kitchen where he'd written in Magic Marker, so the physical evidence of our ordeal had disappeared, but the rest of it was still with us. I had started another afghan, this time in brown and yellow, and was still living primarily on the sofa when I was indoors. Lowell's tirades had become more infrequent but when they exploded it was with new force, and that's the way it would remain between us until we divorced a couple of years later. He never said this, but I suspected that he had a plan to shame me in the hospital, and when it was glossed over by men armed only with bromides, the turmoil within him had become much worse, until it actually seemed to fill the house. This impression was so real to me that as I sat outside with John Lawton, I could sense misery in the building behind me as palpably as I would have sensed a sick animal that I knew was hidden in the bushes.

"I have been thinking that everything will be all right if you can just support your husband more," John was saying to me. That was his magic formula that night, the way the church's explicit sexual code had allowed him to figure out the situation when he came to the hospital. His face as he found the key that would unlock my life was bland and assured.

"I'm sure that would help, Bishop," I said to him.

I have often been asked why I stopped being a Mormon in my middle twenties, when everything I'd done until then had being a Mormon so fiercely at its heart. There isn't one answer to the question—there isn't one thing that *happened*—but there were many things that didn't happen. I didn't storm out of the society that had sheltered and harmed me, didn't fly into a rage at anyone, didn't begin to hate the people who proposed pat answers. There was never a showdown.

There was just a moment when I watched John Lawton's back moving away from me down a quiet street and realized that there was nothing in him that could acknowledge my life's complex circumstances. The rules of our religion were the only rules we knew, he and I, but they were rules that demanded some predictability from days and nights and husbands and wives, and they would no longer stretch to explain my experiences.

I was not very well suited to being alone, but I was completely alone now.

Eight

I

When I walked out of Lowell's house, its pantries still gleaming with my jars of jams, I was traveling at last beyond all my mental pictures. I knew it only dimly and yet I was horrified, since I was unacquainted with the possibility that unexpected events can be glorious. During a lifetime of being influenced, no one had ever suggested such a thing to me.

In fact, just the opposite was true: I had been taught to regard my preordination to a life of Mormon housewifery not as a straitjacket but as the only road to happiness, and ever since I had first left Monty and the plan had derailed, I had sat staring at the wreckage and brooding about the unfairness of the situation. I had kept trying to get back on track, had experienced each uncharted mile as though it were being done to me, a payment extracted for sins I couldn't exactly recall. Every time I had approached a momentous decision I had felt so cornered—had felt forced to marry, then desperate enough to divorce, then desperate enough to remarry and to create my own form of infidelity—that I knew little sense of participation in my own life. All I seemed able to do was to ricochet and to shield my face as I flew into new territory. By now I did not expect the landings to be smooth.

I moved back to Salt Lake City, primarily to be close to

Hannie. I also knew that I was becoming less and less a Mormon, and moving back into the religion's heart was a final convulsion of holding on. From the beginning, that part of my motive didn't work, in that I didn't rededicate myself to the church. I had lost faith, yes. But I also had known with Lowell a misery that was close to horror and had gone beyond the ability to spend my deepest energies forcing myself again and again to do what I thought I should. A person must be fresh for that. Instead, I floated exhaustedly into a society of jack Mormons—those Saints who have forsaken the church's strict standards of behavior or simply never embraced them—because it required so much less of me.

Without admitting it fully, I had been preparing for the transition for some time as, in the years following the moment when I had seen John Lawton with clear eyes, the taboos that had long held my world together had one by one stopped making sense. While I was still with Lowell there had come a day when I could no longer disapprove of his cigarettes; my indoctrination with the church's unbending health code gave way beneath the weight of the thought that although smoking certainly wasn't good for anyone, surely God did not consider something so secular to be a sin.

Then over dinner with a couple of Lowell's friends one evening—an emergency-room physician and a willowy Scandinavian architect who were living together—I had realized that the palpable affection and respect between them was a more honorable bond than the matrimonial vows that held Lowell and me locked in a pattern of twisted retributions. Suddenly I couldn't divorce my judgments of the sex act from my awareness that it was transformed by the heart's intent, and I was titillated and frightened by the change.

Then, watching Lowell sink slowly into a whiskey-soaked sleep on another evening when he couldn't face our marriage and the world, I had finally taken myself off to the kitchen to mix my first drink. I blamed this forbidden act on my husband, telling myself that I needed to learn to drink if I was planning to stay married to him, but even at the time I knew it was a thin excuse. In truth, my stomach was fluttering with excitement as I tipped Lowell's foul-smelling Scotch into a glass, because I couldn't imagine how I was going to be feeling in a few minutes. If you didn't count the tranquilizers I'd gobbled when readying myself to leave Monty, I'd never consumed drugs before, had never even felt curious about them, but apparently my curiosity had only been waiting to peak. I was so overpowered by it now that it nearly crowded out my fear that my virgin tissues would react to alcohol as though it were a hallucinogen, that I would spend the next hours or days imagining that I was covered with insects, or worse.

And I was so ignorant that I filled an iced-tea tumbler half-and-half with water and Pinch and drank it down like medicine. I didn't allow for lag time: When I didn't feel immediately different, I downed another. For the next fifteen minutes I was transported so far beyond daily concerns that I realized the people who claimed to be "high on life" had always been lying, and I passed out right after that. When I awakened six hours later, I'd been put to bed rather tenderly: Lowell had somehow roused himself in order to look after me and had even tucked a towel into the neckline of my nightgown, napkin-style, to protect me from the retching that he'd assumed would accompany my reentry but that miraculously did not. None of that was the biggest surprise, though: As I was discovering that my head had exploded, I was also realizing that the desire to drink was probably rooted most often in the quest for relief, so that its underpinnings weren't so much satanic as deeply human.

Thus it was that by the time I began to make new friends in Salt Lake I was very nearly a jack Mormon in practice, although not ready to see it. I was continuing to slip into church a couple of times a month, sometimes with Hannie. I was continuing to tell my parents over the phone about the pearls of wisdom I was hearing from church leaders in sacrament meeting, not because I was trying to fool them but because I wanted to connect with them. I was flipping through the Book of Mormon occasionally, hoping for instructions that still seemed relevant, and was still praying. But I wasn't a part of it; I simply hadn't let go entirely. And I didn't, until I met Adam Goody and saw a new world I could enter that still linked me to the old one.

I met him through people at work, something I had never been able to say before. Having finally limped through college, I was confronted when I reached Utah with the opportunity to do more with my time than wait for another marriage, which had proved to be an unreliable source of income in any case. The employment I found, although slightly glamorous, wasn't much more reliable: For $750 a month, I was writing and editing at a small city magazine known for its willingness to treat Utah's sacred cows, including the church, with near objectivity.

Although I still viewed working as a temporary thing—it didn't occur to me that I'd embarked upon a career—I found that I was very interested in my job. Beyond my pleasure in having money of my own, which was powerful, I liked talking about, reading about, writing about the social and political issues that underlay my life, all of which were matters to which I'd given little previous thought. And my role at the magazine was also a way to find stability during a major transition: The editor was a round, rebellious, self-reflective man in his forties, a practicing Mormon plagued by doubts, and because I shared an office and soon a blossoming friendship with him, for many hours a day I talked through with a male who wasn't pretending to know the answers the resentments and questions that tormented us both. I'd never known such conversations before, where there wasn't a leader, but soon I knew many more: Most of the other writers possessed lively intellects and relationships with the church that were characterized by disrepair, and both things traveled with them into the saloons where we adjourned after work. After my initial binge, I hadn't taken to drinking very well—I had very little tolerance, and have never tasted Scotch again—but I soon loved sitting around in saloons with my new friends, which is where Adam also sat with his.

I had had a glass or two of wine when he first slid into my range of vision, so I experienced him as though he were surrounded by an enormous aura. Although the visual effects faded with sobriety, my impression of him as a highly romantic figure lasted a decade.

He was quite a small man, and taken a feature at a time he wasn't compelling: His body was slightly chunky and his skin as pale and freckled as my own, and it would have been polite to term him merely "balding." But I couldn't see him a feature at a time, not then and not later. I'm not quite sure who I thought he was that I assigned him such personal power—a radical, perhaps, because upon graduating from Harvard more than ten years before, he had traversed the country in a van with others who staged consciousness-raising sessions and believed they were activists. He was the first person to bring me the sixties.

Or maybe I thought he was a blue-blood, because his parents lived in an exclusive section of the city and owned old silver, and because his father had attended Harvard before him. I knew no one else with such a background. Or perhaps his appeal was that I believed him to be sympathetic but unfettered: His mother's family was a Mormon one, so he knew what I was up against, but his own upbringing had been irreligious. Certainly I didn't see him as he was and is: a bright and caring man who reflects deeply, who is held as fast in the end by Utah's preference for traditional life as though he were himself a priesthood holder. Certainly it never occurred to me that I was the renegade.

We fit together so easily and with such a shared sense of destiny that my fears about secular dating—about the harrowing sexual decisions I had presumed I would have to make now that I could see myself wandering beyond the reach of the church—never really materialized. In light of our intense feelings, not sleeping together was not a serious consideration, even though unmarried sex didn't yet seem like a perfectly good idea to me. The first time we were in bed together, I was about equal parts aware that I'd never before been so close to anyone I loved and ashamed that Adam wasn't my husband, with the result that the emotional aftermath was dramatically uneven. I kissed my first lover good-bye in the wee hours as though trying to take his lips along but then went home and wouldn't answer his calls for days. When I saw him again, I declared that our lovemaking had been a mistake: that I was not the sort of girl for affairs. And then in a few minutes I pulled him onto the bed.

This confusing behavior died down as soon as I'd realized that, whatever my misgivings, I was going to continue to sleep with Adam and that my prissy protestations weren't enhanc-

ing otherwise marvelous occasions. I simply quit telling him
that because I was conflicted and had to summon my courage,
our lovemaking demanded a greater commitment from me
than anything I'd shared with Monty or Lowell.

But my silence didn't mean I was unaware of the thin ice.
Sometimes I woke in the night and watched my lover's face,
and my thoughts strayed to the possibility of living away from
him. I wondered what I'd do with my life without our passion
to hold it together. A few times I crept out of bed and stood
beneath the shower, as though to wash the thought away. I
was afraid I couldn't bear it if Adam fell out of love with me
and, having risked everything including my virtue, I lost.

Losing didn't appear to be an immediate danger, however, and so fear didn't consume me. Excitement certainly did;
I experienced our time together as riotous and daring, particularly once we began living together to some degree in Adam's
eccentric house. Nearly every moment there was one of laughter or discovery that wasn't forced; I had never even imagined
such a pleasure-driven arrangement for myself. However, our
situation was the passionate but still halfhearted one of those
who are in love but hedging their bets; I shared Adam's life
and his bureau space, but I never let the lease expire on my
apartment a few blocks away. My pastel cats lived alone there,
and the apartment became increasingly ghostly beneath the
shroud of hair they shed.

Our close friends were people like us, ex-Mormons or
angry ones or Mormons whose own parents had never been
too devout so that their children's religious conviction was
weaker still. People on the fringes. Like me, many of them
were experimenting. We came together so naturally that I
think, at least in my case, it couldn't have happened otherwise.

It wasn't that the other people I knew in Utah, the

devout ones, had begun overtly to ostracize me; it was that, as I allowed my more liberal thinking to show, there was much unspoken strain and distance between us, on my part as well as theirs. An old girlfriend had become deeply involved during my years away in the cause of denying contraception to teenagers; she spent her days lobbying at the Capitol and then during our luncheons described to me the most scandalous of the legislators—the few who believed that a sixteen-year-old equipped with a condom was the lesser of evils. I was understandably uncomfortable with these stories, and fearful that her rigid judgments would strobe in my direction, and despairing that anything I could say about my own changing morals could be regarded as anything less than my old nemesis Satan whispering to me. I felt that I was waving to my friend from halfway around the world.

Whereas, with the new friends, the instant intimates, it was very cozy. Although they, too, defined themselves in relationship to Mormonism in the valley where the church's interests dictated everything from merchandising to politics, the thing they were always looking at was their distance from the center. Our immersion had been so complete that as we struggled to redirect our lives, Mormonism was still our only gauge. It was true in some way even for those who had never been Mormons, who loved to complain about how difficult it was to get ahead without that all-important affiliation, who told stories about wearing undershirts to job interviews in order to approximate the appearance of garments beneath their clothes.

"Do you still go to church?" we would ask each other.

"Do you believe in the temple . . . the story of Joseph Smith . . . that the Equal Rights Amendment shouldn't pass?"

"Does your family still believe?"

"Do you still wear your garments?"

The answers weren't as important as the ritual of the questions, the acknowledgment that we knew ourselves to be in varying states of falling away. With such admissions we tried to build a new home for ourselves, together. We didn't discuss only religion, but we did cover the Mormon angle every time we got together, in some fashion, as though pressing our lips against a touchstone that took the measure of new friendships and declared ours to be the real thing. Something we could count on as we lost everything else.

Some of our explorations were sweet and trite and funny, as though we couldn't muster more than a slight wickedness as we emerged from institutionalized conformity and innocence. A woman, a writer for the magazine and the wife of a BYU professor, began tearing around town on a motorcycle, her matron's hair tucked into an electric yellow helmet, and she took up belly-dancing. She had played the organ in church since adolescence, a passive assignment, but one Sunday morning she stripped defiantly out of her garments while dressing for Sunday school and then sat elevated at her instrument harboring her delicious secret; she wrote an essay about it called "The Organist Wore No Underwear."

Another wanderer, a man, developed a sudden passion for embraces he claimed were platonic. It was difficult to pass within ten feet of him without being yanked into a lingering hug that was somewhat sexual and far more desperate for connection. Although it was 1980 he could have been an early follower at Esalen; he babbled incessantly about the importance of "human touch," and took to trotting various women into movie theaters in the middle of the day, where he invariably wanted to hold their hands, even when they didn't want to. I never knew of him going farther—he didn't grope the women, or take up drinking, or ask for a puff on anyone's joint—and I got the feeling that after decades in a marriage he still expected would last forever, venturing to clasp the fingers and backs of women he admired was almost more liberation than he could bear.

Sometimes, however, the experiments weren't harmless. I met a man that year who couldn't seem to evaluate anything, not even in the confused, halting way that was common among my new friends: He moved directly from being the leader of his priesthood quorum to encouraging his wife to take a lover in front of him and then weeping while she did. He was a missile of fury streaking away from the church one minute, and in the next a befuddled boy who didn't understand his rash decisions. That was the most radical—the saddest—story I knew; for the most part, as we played along the shores of sexual freedom without considering fully what our yearnings said about our deeper desires to live in more expansive ways, we barely skipped our feet through the most shallow water.

I did my own dabbling in Adam's backyard, in the redwood hot tub that became a site for titillation long after spas filled with naked convivials had become blasé in California. The level of titillation was actually very slight; I don't remember that I was even brushed against accidentally by a naked comrade, and I'm sure no one ever commented to me about my body, although someone once evaluated me for Adam. (Apparently someone told him I had an "elegant hot-tub body," a comment so gentlemanly that it cannot even be interpreted as a leer among men.) I remember a married couple who came to the hot tub and kept themselves always submerged to the neck. The husband squeezed the wife's breasts

lingeringly underwater with as much resolve as though gently
kneading the last drops of juice out of a couple of oranges.
Although he squeezed in full view of everyone, above the level
of these activities his face and his wife's were as formally
conversant and cordial as though we were chatting together
during intermission at the opera. Adam and I kept our faces
similarly composed, as though we didn't suspect our guests.
That was pretty typical of the mood.

Once in a while, I was more at ease than that with
newness, and then I was able to imagine that I had found a
genuine niche. There was a night when we drove into south-
ern Utah with friends, intending to golf over the weekend in
St. George, a town in a majestic red desert that can become
after sunset a terrain of severe shadows and silhouettes cast by
flat-topped mountains. Having checked into our motel, four or
five of us motored through the eerie dark in search of a nearby
natural hot springs, which we finally found bubbling up from
the floor of a cave recessed into a high, red shelf of mountain
that looked straight down upon a river. It was a completely
undeveloped spot except for the little booth at the entrance
where someone took our money. There was only a path, and
the scrubby bushes, and moonlight.

Within the cave it was so dark that as we removed our
clothes we kept running into each other. Someone strummed
his guitar while the rest of us slid silently into the water; a
mournful melody haunted the close space. A bare rump
bumped up against the side of mine and then floated away.
Whatever was in the water empowered it to soften my bones.

Just as I could have drowsed off and drowned, I heard
someone squishing along the floor of the cave in wet flipflops,
and I saw the outline of Adam's body as he stepped through

the mouth of the cave into the wavy moonlight. I followed him, unable to locate my shoes in the dark, and sharp stones cut into my feet.

He was poised at the edge of the rust-colored ledge that ended perhaps twenty feet above the river, standing spotlighted in moonlight so suddenly brilliant that it nearly resembled morning. He was staring into the sky, and his firm, wet, rounded body glistened in the silver light. As he prepared to dive he raised his arms, and the gesture could have been supplication to the gods of the river and the night. His white body streaked into an arc and then exploded into a geyser of foam in the dark river below.

Later that evening, I reached for him as he passed our bed. The door that connected our motel room to our friends' was cracked open, but we were too urgent to give an open door our attention. The timeless illusions of the hot springs were through me like ether as we quietly made love, with so much intensity that I thought I might burn away.

We all went to dinner afterward, and beneath the table Adam kept his hand slipped between my knees. I had never before been sated all at once with the way the earth smelled and with love and sex and food. I thought, I am happy. And then I thought, I am going to have to pay for this.

II

In the autumn of 1980, when Adam and I had been together about six months, the vision began to come and go in my right eye. Gradually an icy numbness crept into the sole of my right foot, and the ends of the fingers on my right hand became deadened until I couldn't distinguish between warm and cool water. Fearful that I'd fallen victim to multiple sclerosis, a silver-haired neurologist punctured the delicate sac surrounding my spinal column and extracted a magical fluid containing the definitive story of my health. It was the story I'd hoped for, and then again it wasn't: I didn't have MS, but the silver-haired neurologist didn't have any idea what was wrong with me, either. Also, the spinal tap had gone awry. As sometimes happens, the needle puncture didn't heal properly and spinal fluid continued to leak. The result whenever I sat or stood was headaches the likes of which I hope never to know again. The doctor said the only cure was to lie completely prone for days on end, until the invisible wound had healed. I wasn't even to use a pillow or sit on the john. I allowed Adam to install me in his big bed, and I began trying to adjust to life from an unvarying perspective.

Those were days spent very distant from the world, defined by sounds and the ways in which others touched me when they entered my animal den. Adam was a very hard-working architect, and after the whoosh of his shower and the sweet pressure of his face against mine, he was off for work early, usually while it was still dark. I heard him sputtering out of the driveway in his faded Fiat and knew that it would be dark again before he returned.

Later I heard the door creaking open as Hannie arrived. She had a key and she came every day while I was ill, to keep me company and empty my bedpans and slide her silky custards down my throat. She brought her two youngest children, who weren't in school yet. The smallest was an infant girl, Carrie, whom Hannie plopped in her carrier onto Adam's side of the bed, close to my head, and who gurgled nearly every moment she wasn't asleep. Her feathery voice trailed after me into my own catnaps and greeted me when I awakened. The four-year-old, Luke, ran through the bedroom's French doors onto Adam's sprawling deck, and the resonant thumps of his feet against planks went on for most of the day.

I had known before I returned to Utah that Hannie had changed, in directions that would allow our friendship to grow rather than create distance. Over the phone, she had a couple of years before stopped being the despairing bride with whom I'd shared the darkest days of my first marriage and had become a vocal wife whose patience with Dickie's abuses was ending. Then when I was barely resettled in Salt Lake City and right after Carrie was born, she had bundled her four kids into the family car and driven them less than three miles to the University of Utah's family housing, where she and the children were to remain for years, until she had completed her Ph.D. program in psychology. I believe that she left both the garage door and Dickie's mouth hanging wide open. Now, during the languid days when being together was our main agenda again, I saw that beneath her life's new set of circumstances, Hannie had combined the new with the old in a way that provided her with support from both.

Unlike me, she was still attending church and pretending to believe when in the presence of believers. As long as I have known her, she has continued to. Perhaps it has been possible for her to maintain a facade because she wasn't exhausted by a divorce that was an ordeal: She was a grown woman when she left Dickie, and many times over a mother, so that she wasn't torn apart by the need to become a virginal girl again, as I was. Certainly her maturity made it a simpler matter for her to endure her own bishop's postmarriage interviews, which had focused, instead of upon sex, upon her bishop's belief that she should return to Dickie. Although Hannie had grown to the point where she found the bishop's interference to be irritating, his line of questioning didn't humiliate her.

But the difference in our reactions was more than a matter of maturity and chance: Something within Hannie had shifted until the teachings of her youth were a comforting ritual instead of a pressure. She had been able to ease up on the church, not to expect anymore that it would fulfill all the promises it had made during her childhood, to see it as only an aspect of her life instead of the foundation. With a wry resignation that was her version of disillusionment, she was untroubled by the afterlife inequities of Mormon divorce and many other things that had torn me asunder before awakening me. She was able to live with ambivalence, perhaps because she focused on the parts of Mormonism that she still loved.

How she milked the traditions for strength and context! She described to me the way that she enjoyed the spirited hymns she still sang on Sundays, loved the mind-blankening experience of pricking her needle endlessly through quilt batting on workdays at Relief Society, even loved (with growing selectivity) the drone of the General Authorities' interchangeable voices during the worldwide conferences that streamed out of the television twice a year. None of which meant that she was content to remain unobtrusive anymore. As much as she gained comfort from her past, she also liked having found her voice.

She had recently been asked to speak in church, in the way that all Mormons are periodically requested to sermonize. In her bishop's eyes, her divorced status didn't disqualify her as a speaker, although I doubt he expected what he got: Hannie had chosen domestic violence as her topic, an issue that, when it is acknowledged at all by General Authorities as a factor in some Mormon marriages, is glossed over at best.

And at worst, the church is blatantly supportive of abusers. (As recently as April 1992, one of the highest leaders of the church, Elder Richard Scott, counseled all victims of abuse—whether physical, emotional, or sexual—to rely upon God's help for healing, and to avoid the "improper therapeutic practice" of "excessive probing into every minute detail of your past experiences, particularly when this involves penetrating dialogue in group discussion." He said that such therapy can "trigger thoughts that are more imagination and fantasy than reality," and can lead to false accusations of abusers. "Remember, false accusation is also a sin," he advised.) From her position on the podium, Hannie embarked upon a consciousness-raising mission: She stared directly into the faces of her ward's husbands and told them how it felt to be manhandled.

"I'm always going to attend church," she said to me. "I think the other members should have the benefit of my viewpoint."

She told other stories, about her new beaux and the sexuality she was quietly allowing herself to discover. Sometimes she spoke with pleasure, as though exploding old values was an activity to be relished a little. "Now that I've had some affairs, I'm not going to sleep with anyone else for a while," she confided. "Some men disappear just when it's getting good. I went out with someone who cried out my name in bed whenever he came, which seemed a very intimate thing. And when he quit phoning me, I realized it was an experience I didn't want to share with very many people I'm not going to know later."

I was very shaken by her strength in the face of change. As the days went by I became aware of the care with which she had extricated herself only from the parts of our culture she couldn't bear, and how firmly rooted this solution had left her. She swept into Adam's house every morning with most of her lifelong sense of herself intact: She was still a mother, a churchgoer, a family member whose bishop phoned her with work assignments, a woman who expected to set up the quilt frames in her living room at least once a year. I saw that the nervous signals of recognition being transmitted back and forth between myself and my new friends could not begin to replace the entire Mormon world I'd lost—that I had no idea whether anything could replace it, and that without it there wasn't a moment in the day when I knew who I was.

I saw, too, that I couldn't embrace Hannie's approach, couldn't inch back into parts of my old world to be soothed and stabilized by its familiarities as though by family recipes. Hannie was able to live the conflict of submitting some part of herself to leaders she didn't respect because of all she felt she gained, but it wasn't an option for me even with a payoff. Although I had eased away from Mormonism without ever meaning to, and by degrees, I hadn't actually left it behind aimlessly. As it turned out, I had embraced the faith from the beginning not primarily because it was all I'd been bred to do, not because it was a life-style, but because I had believed it connected me to God. When my belief in that conduit had died, extinguished by acts and philosophies I came to view as ungodly and the sight of John Lawton's overbroad, uncomplicated back moving away from me down the street, I was too disheartened to remain at the scene of the harm. That was my limit.

Even Hannie had a limit; she discovered it near the end of my confinement, when my restlessness was reaching a peak and her desire to draw me away from my awareness of how achy and unexercised I was feeling may even have contributed to her sudden urge to go to the temple.

She told me the story as soon as she arrived one morning, after she had settled the children into their routine and pulled her chair close to the bed. "I went to an early temple session with my nephew this morning," she announced. "It was his first time through: He's going on a mission."

"How on earth did you get in?" I asked her. I knew that no bishop on earth would have considered her to be "morally clean" at that point in her life.

"I used my sister's temple recommend," she said serenely. "Edie didn't mind; she has absolute trust in me. She said she thought it was all right for me to do so long as I felt I should be there."

She described the Mexican wedding dress she'd worn and portions of the ceremony that I had nearly forgotten. She said that she had loved the washings and anointings. "I do want to be able to participate with my family in the rituals that they consider the very most important," she said wistfully.

Then finally a shadow crossed her face. "I thought I was doing fine until right at the end, when my nephew went through the veil," she said. "And then I looked around at the other members of my family, who were all also watching him, and I knew that we felt immeasurably different about what was happening. It was just too huge a gulf to jump over. The temple is such an extreme place that I can't integrate it into the way I'm living now. I don't think I'll ever go there again."

I realized even at the time how daring Hannie was, suspected that I would never again hear of anyone elbowing into the temple on a false ID, and I haven't. I also realized that I was twice divorced, not a garment wearer, a Friday night imbiber, was living in sin, and yet I couldn't imagine doing such a thing myself. If my conviction that I was a member of the "only true church" had dissolved as Mormonism's guarantees had failed me, some part of me was still afraid to mock the temple ceremony that had once impressed its importance upon me by exacting a promise that I would slit my own throat rather than reveal it. I had slipped away from the parts of my past that had held me up but had not managed to escape one of its major terrors.

Hannie was the free one.

III

My headaches disappeared by the end of the week but the other symptoms, the vision problems and the numbness, were to go on a long time. During the next few years more than one doctor would tell me that my body wouldn't be whole until my mind was, until I had come to terms; one of them would even order a battery of psychological tests that took all day to perform, which he said proved my physical ailments were a symptom of my "lack of inner identity." I didn't believe these doctors (and I also didn't precisely know what "lack of inner identity" meant), but as I've begun to feel more real to myself, my body has gradually returned to normal.

That outcome was still far ahead in the tumultuous weeks and months following my confinement—tumultuous because, as soon as I was on my feet again, I began trying to force my love affair toward a conclusion. Having fully realized how wobbly I was while locked away from thrilling distractions in a dim bedroom, I now demanded that my relationship with Adam shore up my emotional limbo and also my fears that my body was gripped by a serious malady the doctors had yet to diagnose. I was looking for retirement and guarantees. I also really loved Adam, even though my concept of love in those days had much to do with salvation.

We were lounging in our bathrobes on the night I asked him to marry me. Adam's papers were spread all over the dining-room table, where he'd been intermittently taking a stab at applying himself to them, and empty glasses and plates littered the floor by the sofa. There was nothing romantic about the atmosphere, but that room felt to me in my worried state like the only oasis I'd ever know. And so, congratulating myself on being able to take the initiative with a man at last, I asked him.

"My God, my God, I'm just not sure," Adam said. I thought he was declaring that he didn't love me. I couldn't imagine another interpretation to his rejection. Quite as though I hadn't already been battered by two aimless marriages, I still believed that men who truly love their women wish to marry them, and that everyone is happy then.

He did some explaining, to no avail. He said he needed to take marriage slowly, and that my mercurial emotions sometimes made him fear he couldn't keep pace with my changes in mood. He said that he needed more time. His rationale was maddening and sincere and far from fatal, and yet it set our relationship careening down an entirely new course.

I believed that the outcomes I had most feared had happened now: I had gone against my principles to live with Adam and had been cast aside. I had lost my only remaining context. Whatever had been nagging at Adam about my mood changes before he described his doubts, I'm sure it was nothing compared to his perceptions of me afterward. The next months were a time of escalating scenes and confusion and distance. At the end of it, I moved back into my apartment and began to disintegrate.

My close friends knew I had completely lost my bearings, but to much of the world I may have seemed a whirligig of progress, bent on launching out in new directions. It wasn't the case: During the moments when I could pull my thoughts together, I simply began taking desperate stabs at plans that would allow me to leave Utah. Escape was the only coping technique I had ever learned.

Much sooner than I was prepared to handle it, an impulsive application to graduate school resulted in the offer of a fellowship at Northwestern University. It was a marvelous honor but I'd have taken anything. I phoned Adam on the morning I received word and hoped that the reserve in his voice meant that he didn't want me to go, but when he didn't say anything, nothing else could have stopped me. In between crying jags, I sold nearly everything I owned and gave the cats away to a large family who loaded my pets in their cages into the back of a station wagon.

By the day I left for Chicago I was trying to suppress so much misery that I could barely function. I couldn't breathe evenly, couldn't force my mind into the orderly channels that would have allowed me to pack the car in something more livable than a haphazard fashion. Frustrated with the impossible demands of suitcases, I finally began heaping mounds of unprotected clothing onto the hatchback floor of my wine-colored Omni.

That last night I arrived after midnight, uninvited, at Adam's door. We spent six hours together after months apart, trying with alcohol and sex that was thrilling for its desperation to believe in a reconciliation that would stall the knowledge of parting forever. There was still a lot of emotion between us, love and grief and, on my part, anger. Afterward I slept a little, curled against him and holding on.

IV

My mother is a great believer in the ruinability of life. She believes that all lives can be ruined, but when I was growing up she was particularly sure about mine. When I was fifteen, she thought I would ruin my life when she came upon me consuming with relish what she knew to be my second wedge of cherry pie. "If you get fat, you'll ruin your life," she said. When I was sixteen, she saw ruination looming when I broke up with my first steady boyfriend, a close-to-comatose fellow whom my mother had arranged for me to date through behind-the-scenes maneuverings with his mother. When I confessed to her that my boyfriend bored me, my mother said, "If you don't learn to like boys for what they are, you'll ruin your life."

Because she believed that everything a person had worked for could be devastated with one false step, I believed it, too. And yet through nearly a decade of false steps and recoveries, I had managed in time to convince myself that my life wasn't completely ruined yet. It wasn't until I woke up for the first time in the Psychiatric Institute in downtown Washington, D.C., that I ever said to myself, with unassailable conviction, "I have ruined my life."

As I lay in a narrow bed in a cheerless, narrow room, I could see other patients shuffling past the partially opened door. One of them was a middle-aged woman wearing a dress that wasn't outstandingly clean and bedroom slippers she didn't bother to fit entirely onto her feet, so that they were mashed flat at the heels. Her face was as blank as though cleaned by sleep. Another passerby, a young woman, was wheeled past, strapped so tightly to a bed that her arms and legs were imprisoned. I could see the outline of her calves beneath the taut sheets; they were as hard and rounded as stones, as though she were tensing them, which she may well have been. She was thrashing her head frantically from side to side and screaming in a voice that was two parts madwoman and one part monarch. "You son-of-a-bitch fuckers!" she shouted. "I *will not have it,* do you hear? You murdering cunts! Do you think this will do it! *It won't do it!* You're all murderers!"

The place was called PI by its inmates, sometimes affectionately. A private hospital with a reputation for innovation, it took up several floors of an office building in a good section of the heart of the capital city. I often sat at the picture window on the fourth floor and stared at Washingtonians rushing past below, dressed in loafers and low pumps and every imaginable wardrobe item that can be sewn in khaki, and I wished that I could stroll with them into the cafés and bookstores that littered the district. These yearnings filled me because I had the feeling while at PI that I had not so much gone there to get well as just disappeared into it forever.

My grip on reality had begun to loosen in Illinois, when I arrived at graduate school. As though acting out my complete loss of moorings, I had proved incapable in Evanston of learning my way back and forth from the student news service in downtown Chicago. From day to day I couldn't remember the name of my "el" stop; I usually couldn't even remember that the commuter train was referred to as the "el." As the quarter progressed, so did the problem: I had so much trouble retaining new information that I stayed up all night before my media-law final, not to study but because I was afraid that in sleep the material I'd learned so painstakingly would slip through my brain like sugar coming through a strainer.

I had been in Washington for two weeks, reporting to work every day at the student-staffed news service that NU maintained downtown as the next phase of the graduate journalism curriculum, when I couldn't seem to go any farther. A mixture of fatigue and profound confusion brought me to my knees; I hardly remember the last couple of days. I located a doctor through the Yellow Pages and confessed to him that I couldn't pull myself together. He wrote out a prescription for Elavil and I overdosed on it partially as a reflex, as the next thing to do rather than struggle to find the Metro station one more time. As I drowsed off, indescribably lonely despite the numbing action of the drugs, I raged at Adam with my last thread of consciousness for letting me down and driving me to this.

A terrified classmate (someone who never forgave me) found me and deposited me at PI, where I was placed into the hands of a deceivingly gentle psychiatrist named Dr. Handle. He was a fortyish black man whose English was halting and grammatically inexact, and the first non-Mormon psychiatrist I'd ever known. If he was close to inarticulate, he nonetheless possessed clamorous radar when in the presence of self-deception. With a benign smile and a nod and a few garbled words, he agreeably called me on every con during countless therapy sessions.

When I complained that the floor's other inmates seemed genuinely crazy to me, whereas I perceived myself as merely depressed, he asked, "Aren't you scared really that you're sicker?"

When I waved off, as though I'd expected it, Adam's refusal to fly to Washington for the joint therapy sessions that Dr. Handle thought might help me to move on, he said, "I think this hurts you terrible."

And whenever his sharp truths nicked into the quick of my denials and reduced me suddenly to relieved and bewildered tears—What was this sweet, healing pain I was feeling?—he smiled and nodded behind his twinkling spectacles as though I were the insightful one in the room. "Now you beginning to unpeel like an onion," he would say.

After more than eight years of morals lectures from therapists who believed themselves to be General Authorities, he was my first exposure to the idea that telling myself the truth about my feelings was more important to my future than hearing the rules in ever-greater detail.

Dr. Handle interred me on the PI ward known as "the community," a group of forty patients who were forced to share everything—thoughts, complaints, responsibilities—even though rendered completely incapable of pleasantly doing so by their all-absorbing illnesses. We met together in the recreation room the first thing every morning, and I for one listened with amazement while the staff members traced aloud the slightest signs of everyone's progress and decline. "Elizabeth had a fight with her mother yesterday, and a bad night," they would say. Or, "Josh is going to be starting on a new medication this afternoon, and will need your extra support." We would all turn then and stare at Elizabeth and Josh with a complete lack of sympathy. We had our own problems.

Upon my groggy arrival at PI I had asked—had practically demanded—to be assigned to a room, or even another hospital, where I could undergo only one-on-one therapy, but Dr. Handle had outright refused. He had said my rehabilitation depended upon seeing "the reality of others' lives." I didn't know what he meant by this, but to the extent that I understood it I hated the idea. I couldn't imagine that I would be healed by observing the weirdos wandering around the ward like the animated pages of an encyclopedia about aberrant life.

But I was wrong.

That was the summer when I witnessed a grown man confessing his homosexuality to his mother with terror in his voice, when I saw the mother's face struggling in every crease for acceptance.

I watched a woman who entered the hospital chuckling that she and her husband were still so in love that they had pet names for each other's sex parts admit finally to everyone that her husband had left her the previous year.

I made friends with a beautiful brown-eyed fifteen-year-old, Blake, whose father, a squatty military man, was so outraged by his son's depression that he railed in front of the entire community that the boy was just feeling sorry for himself. Eight days after Blake was forced by his father to leave the hospital, I sat with a group of fellow patients in the hall, and received the news that my friend had drowned himself in the Potomac.

I saw, in short, that the world was filled with people with serious adjustments to make instead of Mormonism's mythical, serene, and smiling families, and I saw those troubled people struggling hellishly to erect lives for themselves unlike anything they had once imagined. I saw that the effort of it and the fear of never finding understanding had made them ill—that I wasn't alone or outrageously weak because the same thing had happened to me when I was confronted with starting from scratch.

That, at least, is what I learned from the patients who

seemed on some level to be just like me—stopped in their tracks but headed back, in time, into relatively normal lives. There was another category, the patients like Melody and Eugenie, who were possessed by lunacies, who were in the end my greatest teachers.

This was true partially because at PI I was ready to change. As I had tried to keep matching my life's events to my first assumptions, it had never been the case before. Now I was both desperate and genuinely broken down, the emotions of the juncture where the mind can become a precise instrument for metaphor. I was able to see in front of me the exact symbols of the things I needed to know. Of course, I hardly could have missed these particular symbols. At PI, the sign-posts for change were too exaggerated to ignore.

Melody was a good-natured black woman of about thirty who worked as a secretary to a minor government official. She was pretty and padded—not fat but wonderfully rounded, so that her voluptuousness was the first thing you noticed. As if her name were also her destiny, she possessed a speaking voice so musical that I could often hear it tinkling beneath the babble of talk on the ward.

She seemed remarkable in the beginning primarily because she wasn't remarkable, was so smiling and normal and unmedicated in appearance that in the weeks before I realized that most of PI's inmates were simply sufferers and not schizo-phrenics, I wondered why Melody was among us. I found myself watching her during the morning meetings the way I might have kept coming back to the single calm child in a roomful of tantruming ones. But this initial impression didn't last.

I was outside my room one night, rocking back and forth

in a lobby chair and crying. (At the beginning of my therapy I cried because I couldn't believe I would ever leave—whenever I threatened to check myself out, Dr. Handle threatened in his smiling way to commit me. Later I cried because I was beginning to confront the ideas within me that weren't working, and to get well.) My sniffling stopped abruptly when Melody suddenly reared up in front of me. I say "reared" because she paused unexpectedly for a long look directly into my face on her way down the hall, which she had been prancing down as though she were a horse. This is not a figure of speech: Melody was decked out in her ladylike pink slippers and robe, but she really thought she was a horse. After a few moments she swung her head around slowly, as though it were on the end of a very long neck, and set off again, this time stepping very high. She'd gone only a few steps when she let out a long whinny. She whinnied very well.

I had been witnessing quite a lot during the days immediately prior to this one, but Melody as a horse was unusual even at PI. I set my own grief aside and followed her down the hall. She turned into the bathroom and, perhaps because she was a horse and horses don't have hands, she neglected to shut the door. I watched from the doorway as she dropped onto all fours and bent to drink out of the toilet. She did so with a marvelous familiarity; she snorted, she put her head right into the bowl. She turned to look at me once in exactly the momentary, inscrutable way an animal watches when you come into its line of vision at mealtime. And then one of the psychiatric workers located her and led her past me and away to her room.

Melody told us about her adventure at the morning meeting; it seemed that her equine period had been just the beginning of a psychotic delusion that lasted most of the night. She confided that she couldn't avoid such episodes whenever she allowed herself to slack off on her medication, which she invariably did as soon as she began to feel better. This was her umpteenth visit to the hospital to stabilize, but in the meantime she was having a wild ride. As she said all this she paused frequently to laugh, and her laughter sounded genuinely well adjusted.

I watched Melody even more closely after that, amazed that she never appeared to be disconsolate about her illness and visions, not when they gripped her and not afterward.

It didn't appear, either, that she had become ill as a result of her life collapsing around her. Many of the other patients lurched through therapy histrionically, staging huge scenes with husbands and mothers during family therapy sessions and having to be isolated afterward in the tiny white room right by the nurse's station that knew the constant ebb and flow of the most imminently suicidal among us. Melody, however, was visited only by her sister, and they sat together so uneventfully that they could have been elderly women bound together by so many excellent memories that there was no need for talk.

I have often heard it said that the insane are happier than the sane, invariably by someone who hasn't spent any time with psychotics. Everyone I knew at PI whose head was rented to demons was distraught about it during lucid moments, except for Melody. Perhaps she was distraught as well; perhaps she was denying her true feelings. But I didn't see any denial; I saw her finding amusement and almost contentment within an inner world without boundaries. Because of her lack of grief, she began to seem to me like a woman of unfettered imagination whose options were endless. I had grown up seeing only a few sorts of lives based upon a few narrow choices, and I'd become ill when I'd felt my own puny options and even their rebellious opposites had been exhausted—that I had failed as a Mormon and even a jack Mormon, as a wife and even a forbidden lover. But now I began to suspect that my life wasn't really over.

One day I was sitting in the hallway with Melody and a twenty-five-year-old manic depressive named Parley. This is what we did when we weren't huddled together during group therapy: We lounged in the halls and lobbies and rec room and we discussed our illnesses. We also discussed our pasts as they had contributed to our illnesses and our futures as they might affect our illnesses later.

Parley had spent more than half his life in mental hospitals in search of the magical balance of chemicals that would allow him to live normally. During a manic phase he had once danced the night away, barefoot, until he literally wore the skin off the soles of his feet. He didn't feel manic very often, though; in the main he was terribly depressed. Since he'd gone on lithium his chances for a serene life had greatly improved, but even that hadn't been a final answer: Parley slacked off on the drug with the sort of frequency that suggested the hospital was a home to which he longed to return.

That day, Melody was recounting a story in which she had spent much of the previous night dressing and undressing in fascination because her hallucination was causing her to think she was white, and Parley's reaction to her reminiscence was entirely apprehensive. "Weren't you scared?" he kept asking her, his voice nearly hoarse with vicarious doom. "Weren't you afraid you'd have to be white forever?"

"No," Melody told him. "I'm not one of those black people who has always yearned to be white, but on the other hand, I thought that being white would be very interesting."

It is the hardest thing in the world to see beyond the walls of your personal universe, or even to imagine anyone else doing it, but I saw it happen then. Suddenly I was crying huge, relieved sobs that began to empty my intestines of pain. I cried for a long time, seeing the problem, wanting to also perceive my world fearlessly as one of ever-widening possibilities.

V

Eugenie was my favorite person at PI, in time. She was my roommate for a while, and after I got to know her she seemed, at thirty, more highly educated than anyone I'd ever met. Her father, a well-known painter who during the weeks of his daughter's confinement was mounting a gallery show in Europe, had been spoon-feeding her with the most delicious morsels of culture since birth, and perhaps it was the exposure to all of life's most refined aspects that had resulted in her very serious nature. I had never before seen anyone regard each moment as though there were quite so much at stake. Eugenie was a nervous wreck.

She was also large and, in the beginning, very unkempt. She came to us accompanied by her mother, as I believe she was always accompanied by her mother. The mother was small and dark and tight-faced, and when I first saw her she was wearing spectator pumps and a long, plain, dark dress that badly needed ironing. She was fluttering along behind her much taller daughter like a slightly frowsy, nervous fashion coordinator trailing a prized model who had allowed herself to go hopelessly to seed.

"I have brought your special face soap and your washcloth from home," she was saying sternly. "Don't neglect your skin while you're here. You know what happens."

It was Eugenie's mother who first arranged Eugenie's toilet articles on the nightstand in our little room while Eugenie herself sat on the edge of her bed staring straight ahead, apparently deaf and unseeing. Her feet tapped out a furious rhythm on the floor. Suddenly she blurted, "What should I do now?," and her voice was frantic and quavery.

As though her daughter hadn't spoken, Eugenie's mother continued to fuss with hairbrushes and toothbrushes. Finally she took Eugenie by a fleshy upper arm and led her off to another part of the ward.

I saw them again later, seated close together in the hall. Eugenie's mother was nodding decisively, as though to punctuate a lecture. "Remember about your food allergies," I heard her say as I passed.

I never got completely clear on the nature of Eugenie's disorder. Staff members were hesitant to explain anyone's diagnosis in detail, and Eugenie herself offered only unintelligible explanations in the beginning. Then when she began to recover, she bore herself with such an air of dignified reserve that I hated to press her. (I did once hear a nurse say as an aside, "That woman's mother is her problem.") So if I knew nothing about her condition when we parted, I knew far less during our first evening together, when much was expected of me.

I had barely drowsed off that night when Eugenie sat straight up in her bed and let out a wail like a desolate animal's. "What should I do *now*?" she wanted to know, the same question I had earlier heard her pose to her mother.

At first I roused and applied myself to the problem fully

as though it were a real one. What was she asking me for exactly? I wanted to know. Wasn't she feeling well? Or was she just unable to sleep and seeking activities to help her drift off?

This approach didn't work. "What should I do?" Eugenie began repeating, with increasing panic. Disillusioned with rational assessment, I padded out to the nurse's station to retrieve the psychiatric worker who was on night shift. When he had led Eugenie into the hallway and the shrill sound of her demands for guidance was receding, I gratefully fell asleep again.

And was again awakened. This time Eugenie was standing over me, chanting and shaking me by the shoulders. Apparently she had been allowed to return to bed once she had quieted down. "What should I do *now*?" she wailed.

I decided that I needed to be firmer with the psychiatric worker. I stalked out to his station and recommended that he try harder to help the girl. "Don't let her fool you; she's in no mood for sleep," I told him.

But apparently I did not get through to him. "What should I do *now*?" Eugenie was soon crying again from the bed next to mine. She was beginning to pose the question with so much textured anguish that it fell on my ears like a query about the nature of the human condition.

It was getting very late and they convened the morning meetings very early, so I really wanted to come up with something. I thought the situation over while Eugenie worked herself up to a rolling boil.

Finally I said, "Turn over in your bed and go to sleep. Sleep until morning."

The room fell so suddenly silent that it was as though Eugenie had given up on everything in the middle of her worst moment, and had died. Then there was a heaving sound as she rolled her big body away from me toward the far wall, and very soon I could hear only the whistle of her even breathing. She had just been looking for any sort of leader. If I'd said, "Singe all your eyebrows off," she'd have spent the night roaming the halls in search of matches. This girl was caught in a faltering syndrome that was no way to live.

And that, to only a slightly lesser degree, was my own syndrome: I realized that Eugenie was a pitiful, comical carica-ture of me. I, too, had always expected someone else to point out my next move. In fact, the only difference between Euge-nie and myself during the critical moment that had just solved everything was that I had tried *something,* anything. I hadn't assumed there was a perfect answer that only someone who was less likely than me to make a mistake could know—the psychiatric worker or a bishop or Dr. Handle or Adam. I hadn't assumed that things would work out nicely if I did nothing more than drift into the next moment without making too big a fuss.

I lay beside my new mentor in the dark, feeling my chest opening and my future falling into my hands, wondering what else I was capable of.

VI

It took me a long time to get well, to understand to the point of acting on it that I have a perfect right to work out my life as best I can, in ways that may not constitute final answers but that appeal to me and move me slightly forward. I needed to know I have a right; when I was with Adam and his friends, it wasn't enough to see the adventure of charting a new course as the only thing left to me.

And as I began to make my own choices I began to learn to find good fits. I discovered that I am sustained by the moments and the people that aren't easily explained—the complex, the quirky, the unconventional. These things imbue my view of the world with texture and delight. I often wonder how I lived so long believing that sameness and obedience were the greatest virtues, lived in a universe replete with mystical weirdness but no real oddness where I might have altogether overlooked someone like Parley, who changed my life.

I didn't see it as a landmark at the time, but in one way I walked into the second part of my life near the end of my eight weeks at PI, on the night I taught Parley to dance.

The evidences of Parley's peculiar life in hospitals hung from him everywhere, like clothing. Some of the evidence *was* clothing, in that he had long outgrown most of his but couldn't afford or didn't bother to replace it. His bony wrists and big feet jutted out of his cuffs and his pant legs, and nearly everything about him emphasized this ungainly image: He was tall and loose, his hair was badly cut, and for some reason his neck and ears were often as red and raw-looking as though they'd just been scrubbed clean by an impatient mother. If not a dashing figure he was an adaptive one, however, with well-developed hormones, so that he had transformed the institutions where he spent his time into the exact surroundings he needed—his personal equivalent of singles bars. Parley didn't allow the fact that he was meeting only pathologically depressed women to thwart his quest for romance, although his approach kept him from getting very far. For instance, he moved on me toward the end of my stay by declaring, ''You're kind of pretty, but I've never noticed it before because you were always crying."

I wasn't interested in Parley's interest, but when I told him so it was gently, because I had come to feel very protective toward him. Protectiveness was a new feeling for me in relationship to a man, as many things were beginning to feel new. I had often watched him loping down the hall, awkward as a gosling, and had filled unexpectedly with the hope that he'd find his way back into the real world. I had been aware that I had not very many times before felt affection for a man that wasn't based upon my need for him. So Parley was already rather dear to me on the night he declared himself, and as we sat together afterward in the rec room I found myself wanting, just once before I left PI, to relate to him on a basis that wasn't patient-to-patient.

And so we agreed that I'd teach him to dance. As we had passed the time at PI listening to records, I had often heard him bemoan his ignorance of dancing, the activity that comes more naturally to me than any other. I had never followed up on it because the staff discouraged us from touching each other at PI, undoubtedly because of eager and woundable patients like Parley. "Can you handle it?" I asked him frankly. "Can you dance with me knowing I'm getting out of here next week and that you won't see me again?" And when he said he could, I decided that I could recognize a proper occasion for going against regulations.

We plotted the lesson under our breath for days, and finally crept along the hall toward the rec room at two in the morning. The staff members didn't notice us because they were thinned out and unsuspecting at that hour, and gathered behind the half-closed door of their sacred lounge.

When we reached the rec room, we didn't dare turn on

the lamps or turn the stereo up loud. We made do with the light from the hall, which melted the chairs and tables closest to the door into creepy silhouettes and didn't extend at all into the farthest reaches by the record player. We muffled the music until the voice of Emmy Lou Harris was only a tinny buzz. We stood together in the complete dark and put our arms around each other shyly.

Almost immediately, Parley began thudding and sliding across the floor so resoundingly that I began to fear discovery. "This isn't a polka!" I hissed at him. "Just shift your weight in time to the music." My partner thus subdued, we began to creep around a little cleared space in the room.

Beneath the fabric of his shirt, I could feel that his back muscles were knotted into lumps that filled my palm and felt permanent. I imagined that no one had ever massaged his back; that his was a life where no one touched him. Why else would he be trembling slightly, as though the experience of being touched by a woman completely unnerved him? Why else would he hold his hand so rigidly where it lay curved into the small of my back, as though the slightest movement might remind me it was there and cause me to ask him to remove it?

He was breathing through his mouth, from excitement or his earlier exertion. His breath smelled very sweet, as though he'd been chewing on grass. He didn't try anything.

As we inched around the dance floor together, it was an unimaginable thing. I could never have predicted that I would one day insist upon dancing secretly with a misfit like Parley. I couldn't have known that I would find in myself the kind of respect I was feeling for this struggling man who had poured his lifetime supply of energy not into preparing for godhood but into merely getting up in the morning. As I had never admired anything, I admired that morning after morning he was continuing to get up.

I held him, and wasn't frightened to have not foreseen this night. I welcomed everything that was unfamiliar into my arms.

Epilogue

I return to Salt Lake City nearly every year. I have dear friends there, comrades from the Adam period as well as Adam himself, who has turned out to be that unusual person whom I will always know, perhaps because the bond is a strong one when you have vastly disappointed each other and found that there is still a connection.

I also have a feeling of homecoming when I drive in at night from the airport and come upon the magically illuminated temple. It took me years to regain the latter, to realize that I can embrace some symbols of my upbringing and still have moved away from it. Now I marvel again at the massive cathedral that dominates downtown like a haunted castle. The early Saints built the temple for forty years with their bare hands; they hauled the finest granite from nearby canyons for the House of the Lord while living in log cabins themselves. They taught me that it is hard work to be a pioneer.

I see my life today—as a single woman, a writer and newspaper executive, and a valued member of a group of tight-knit friends—as being a nineties version of pioneering, even though I know that to the devout from my past it may appear to be my punishment for falling away. I realize that many people who once believed I held promise cannot imagine that I am finding happiness as a childless, unmarried woman on the threshold of forty, and that those things I regard as my best accomplishments—my joy in my career, my intense friendships, and my hard-won mental health—are easily discounted by them. ("I always knew that you'd do well at whatever you pursued; it's just that I expected you to pursue different things—church and family," my brother Len said to me recently, and there was no mistaking the gentle reproof in his voice, the sentiment that much of my time has been wasted.) At a family party, surrounded by pretty nieces in their twenties who are already jostling several babies apiece, it is possible for me to feel invisible.

But it's an outgrown feeling now, a reflex that bubbles up and frustrates me and then settles down, largely replaced by my desire to live in ways I haven't experienced, that were unavailable to me for nearly thirty years, because I either wasn't aware of them or thought I shouldn't reach for them:

I want to eschew what's superficial among people, and I believe that most of a "traditional life," certainly a traditional Mormon life, occurs only on the surface, where denial of fears and doubts is possible. Instead, I want to talk meaningfully and honestly with those I love about how we perceive ourselves and our friendships.

I want to be free to draw no conclusions at all about the nature of God without feeling that my inability to know Him now is a lack of faith.

I don't want to fear I'll be corrupted by everything that's different; I want to search the unfamiliar and threatening for what they have to teach me.

I want to care for a man without needing him or even needing to admire him, and certainly without believing he is my ticket to heaven; I want love that grows out of a fearless affection for imperfection and reality instead of religious illusions.

I want pleasure and hope and understanding that is broader and richer than I knew or could know while others called the shots in the name of God, when I was allowed to embrace a point of view that flowed in only one direction.

I want all these things that weren't available in Mormonism, and I particularly want to make my own energetic mistakes instead of failing through default or desperation. My third marriage was one of those mistakes, and I learned a great deal from it.

I left PI nearly twelve years ago and married Lewis a few years later, at the conclusion of a courtship that made up in grand gestures whatever it lacked in length. He was a smart, brash, hugely charming lawyer with more flair than discretion, who wooed me with beautiful letters, flowers that overflowed the house, and constant declarations that we were meant for each other in which God's name never once arose, to my relief. I loved the way he filled every room without seeming to crowd me, and he loved my intelligence and the way my career was launched by then, so that I wasn't basking in the light of his successes. We were married three months to the day after our first dinner date, on a balcony of San Francisco's Mark Hopkins Hotel, during a moment when I believed I was embarking upon the most romantic journey of my life. That ceremony was a heartfelt one where the others had been forced, a union forged between two people in their right minds who both wanted it to happen.

But enthusiasm wasn't enough. I had grown sufficiently at last to decide upon marriage for myself, but I couldn't make this completely secular marriage work. I think it was similar for Lewis: Faced with getting to know and accept each other, we didn't know how. When we finally admitted it and parted with sadness and confusion, each of us haltingly resumed our singular lives without blasting apart into shrapnel, however; even while we were together, during the very worst of it, we treated ourselves and each other with some respect. For me, that was one of the primary differences in a marriage that wasn't about Mormonism: When we didn't succeed, the disappointment had a human scale. All of heaven and earth wasn't at stake, and we weren't compelled to endlessly point fingers and punish each other.

That was its grace but there was a footnote: Without the formidable Mormon temple beckoning, luring me with the promise of entrance to the most exalted heaven, I didn't know what marriage signified and I didn't embrace it in the same dogged way that demanded I nearly destroy myself rather than leave. Although I didn't believe anymore that the purpose of marriage was to form a family for the afterlife, I didn't know what else to believe. What sort of commitment was this? I wondered. Were we together for better or worse but not for lousy? Without religious ropes binding us together, I often didn't feel tethered at all.

I realized that I was ignorant of the willing commitments that grow out of nothing more forced than friendship, but that I wanted to know about them. In the years since I've been single again, only such commitments have drawn me; I've ceased to see marriage as a goal.

Instead, I've found joy and stability among friends, the handful of men and women who share with me the great and small details of their lives and always want to know mine. I've been surprised by the depth of intimacy these well-tended friendships have provided, the extent to which I now depend upon loving and being loved without fear of losing. That is the constant: The friendships themselves are very different from each other. My work has brought me back to Phoenix, and my house here is cradled between two of the most abiding friends, who live slightly to the north and south and provide me with a strong sense of family. With others I share a deep attraction to literature and ideas; with still others, a fascination for the way society is put together and a desire to examine its underside, the passion that has also held me fast in the world of journalism. And I have now known long romances with friends, as well—years at a time when I've been opened entirely to another person purely because of the affection between us. These have been very satisfying periods, and the rehabilitation continues. I really don't know what's next.

It is a very simple formula—I'm constantly in touch with people I love and I'm profoundly involved with work I love. It doesn't fill up every emptiness, but it steadies me and allows me to hope that doors will continue to open.

It is probably true these days that I am buttressed and befriended more profoundly by my work and the "family" I have built for myself than by the family I was born into, but that isn't to say that my parents and brothers and I have shunned each other as our beliefs have diverged. My parents in particular have striven to accept without censure every change I've made; there has been hardly a moment when I haven't felt completely welcome in the home I still return to. They are not "liberal" Mormons. They walk in near-lockstep with the dictates of the church leaders, so when I see them continuing to reach out to me I know it's not an effortless gesture. With my brothers there is peace, and Ernest has even assured me that he quit fearing for me once he saw that I'm not rudderless—that I am still guided by moral principles he recognizes.

Nonetheless, there is a great distance between us that no one acknowledges aloud or ever for a moment escapes. I suspect that for my parents it is a wide river of sadness, the belief that I have forfeited my place in their eternal family and will not belong with them after death. And between all of us there lies the edgy knowledge, despite our love for each other, that we are nothing more than polite about the other's primary choices—that I have not simply gone off in another direction in their eyes but have apostasized, have betrayed all they stand for. That to me they are not merely faithful members of a major church that I would rather not attend, but are caught up completely in a repressed social movement that discourages them from thinking for themselves. We don't talk about it because we can't and stay intact, so we do the best we can; we offer each other goodwill and very little real understanding.

As my relationships with my family members have necessarily narrowed, my relationship with God has only broadened, however. I see Him everywhere and am content for His true nature and purpose to be a mystery. As I have noticed that even I am more unlimited than I'd supposed, I've come to understand that I can't begin to fathom His breadth anyway; I have wondered why so much of the world's energy is squandered in trying. Is He a spiritual being or human being, a father or a friend? Does He watch over me? Is He attended by a cavalcade of spirit messengers? Does He think in terms of sin? I watch others wrestle with these questions and am bewildered. Surely whatever great power organized our intricate world didn't do so as an exercise in ego; surely our success in it isn't contingent upon correctly defining and worshiping Him. I am just grateful to feel His strength whenever I feel my own; I sense that the part of me that's quiet and clear-eyed is in touch with the divine.

While I've been changing, the Mormon Church hasn't remained static, although its philosophical shifts haven't been as dramatic as mine. In what may have been an attempt to meet the demands of twentieth-century women, the rules for eternal marriage were changed in 1990. As though unable to grant true equity, the General Authorities' new views on the subject are primarily confusing, however: A woman now may also be "sealed" in the temple to more than one man, but the circumstances must be special. If she has lost a first, "sealed" husband through death or divorce and she remarries civilly, her relatives may, following her death, arrange for a proxy temple "sealing" that will join her in the afterlife to her second husband as well. Men still do not have to fool with any of this rigamarole: They may be "sealed" to multiple wives while still alive to follow through for themselves.

The church public information officer who explained this to me recently, a very polite man named Joe Walker, sounded as bewildered about it as I was feeling. Why is there still such a difference, and what does it all mean about how men and women will live in heaven? I asked him.

"That is just the way it is," he said, his voice colored with a slight misery that may have been embarrassment. "This is not something we decided for ourselves; it was accomplished through revelation. There is quite a lot about this 'sealing' process that we don't really know."

There are other changes—more straightforward ones. It is no longer automatic that those who are divorcing are barred from the temple, and the temple ceremony itself was radically altered in 1990 in ways that relieved moderns and feminists. The horrifying "penalties" of throat slitting and heart gouging that had unnerved me as a bride were eliminated, and women now make their covenants directly to God instead of to their husbands.

In a way that signifies how the General Authorities are more unbending than ever with their millions of followers and that the temple's covert mysticism still reigns supreme, however, these changes were accompanied by trauma.

Church officials refused comment to the media about the loosened rules, saying that it is church policy to not discuss its sacred ceremonies. When word leaked into the national press anyway, a Salt Lake City magazine, *Sunstone,* published a summary of the news stories. In response, church officials rescinded the temple recommends of *Sunstone's* editor and publisher.

One prominent church member who did take a reporter's call was Ross Peterson, a professor of history at Utah State University. Not only was his recommend recalled as a result, but he was threatened with excommunication by church leaders. Although Peterson had only praised the church to the Associated Press for its new liberalism, he says that ecclesiastical high-ups summoned him to a private meeting and chided that he had shown himself throughout the years to be resistant to church authority, an excommunicable offense. To prove their point, his leaders waved in front of him a dossier containing materials collected since the sixties that documented his activism in the Democratic party, that quoted him in his professional capacity as a historian—even a letter to a hometown editor that presumably demonstrated Peterson didn't believe church leaders are inspired. Peterson, himself a former bishop, was not intimidated and in time prevailed: His recommend was restored and the excommunication threat was silenced.

The incident does more than answer the question I asked myself long ago when first cautioned in the temple that I should share its goings-on with no one: "What would they do to me?" It stands as one among many examples of the heavy-handed way in which church leaders are disciplining those whom they consider to be dissidents, particularly church intellectuals who criticize Mormonism in the press or through other writings. More and more, modern-day leaders are insinuating themselves into every aspect of members' lives while trying to mask their real intent: Like old-time Soviet dictators euphemizing tyranny by referring to their subjects as "comrades," they have labeled the brethren assigned to gather information on subversives as the "Strengthening Church Members Committee." When, in light of the Ross Peterson incident and others, the committee was challenged in the summer of 1992 by "liberal" Mormons seeking reform, the church's response made headlines: Leaders claimed that their tracking paranoia was scripturally based, and trotted out a long passage from the Doctrine and Covenants, a collection of Joseph Smith's revelations that Mormons regard as seriously as the Book of Mormon.

"We would suggest for your consideration the propriety of all the saints gathering up a knowledge of all the facts, and sufferings and abuses put upon them by the people of this State," Smith had written in 1839. "And also the names of all persons that have had a hand in their oppressions, as far as they can get hold of them and find them out. And perhaps a committee can be appointed to find out these things, and to take statements and affidavits; and also to gather up the libelous publications that are afloat; And all that are in the magazines, and in the encyclopedias, and all the libelous histories that are published, and are writing, and by whom, and present the whole concatenation of diabolical rascality and nefarious and murderous impositions that have been practised [sic] upon this people."

What the General Authorities didn't mention is that Smith's instructions had been directed to church members at the height of the violent persecutions of the early Mormons that drove them from state to state, tarred and feathered them, burned down their temples, murdered Smith himself and others, and ultimately made an evacuation to the unsettled West and the brutal hardships involved in relocation seem like a glittering opportunity. In fact, at the time this "revelation" was received, Smith was a prisoner in Liberty, Missouri: He wrote these instructions from his jail cell, directing the members of his flock to keep their eyes upon the outsiders who were threatening their very lives. His know-thine-enemy doctrine was about self-preservation, a far cry from today's McCarthy-esque tactics, which find church members spying upon each other internally with no more provocation than a distaste for every opinion that's not the party line.

The silencing or incapacitating of Mormons who question the pronouncements of modern authorities seems to me the logical progression of attitudes for priesthood leaders like those who sanctioned me for nothing, who were smug or patronizing or bullying or unhearing.

And as the years have passed, I have seen this institutionalized complacency directed not only toward intellectuals and dissidents but toward the women who, unlike me, have directly challenged church authority. The most infamous example was the excommunication of Mormon housewife Sonia Johnson, who in 1979 was banished for her support of the Equal Rights

Amendment and her zeal to publicly reveal that the church was covertly organizing nationwide to defeat it. If the Johnson affair ballooned into a public-relations fiasco for the church, however, embarrassment has not lessened leaders' resolve to keep the church's women acquiescent and homebound. As recently as 1987, Ezra Taft Benson declared that "contrary to conventional wisdom, a woman's calling is in the home, not the market-place." In the spring of 1992, General Authority Dallin Oaks—the president of BYU during part of the time I attended there and now one of the most precisely unbending leaders—celebrated the 150th anniversary of the women's auxiliary, the Relief Society, with a public address whose entire point was to rebut the Mormon feminists who are clamoring to hold priesthood power: In no uncertain terms, he reminded them that the Relief Society is not autonomous but is controlled and directed by male priesthood leaders.

The vast majority of members agree with such senti-ments, and those who don't agree may feel the pain: A well-known law professor and Salt Lake City Mormon, a man who lobbies that women should be allowed to hold the priesthood, recently received death threats after declaring publicly, "I long for that time when four black people, three of them women, will sit on the stand as General Authorities." And Karen Case, one of the founders of the Mormon Women's Forum—a group of "liberals" crusading for women to be ordained to the priesthood—as a result was disfellowshiped, a punishment that stops short of excommunication but that stripped Case of the right to participate in Mormon sacraments.

Despite the repercussions, those who love the Mormon Church but want to change it continue to speak out. Now when I visit Utah, I often come upon "liberal" Mormons—that small minority of men and women who question the leaders openly, or who don't accept the church's supernatural origins, or who call for modernization of doctrine and other reforms.

Perhaps I get to know these naysayers because it is easy for us to talk together, whereas with the staunch Mormons I have known there is practically no common ground, even in everyday things. My final devout girlfriend, the one who had adopted as her cause the contraceptive practices of teenagers, seemed uncomfortable to see me a few years back when I dropped by the sprawling, immaculately tended house in the Salt Lake City hills that had once been a second home to me. Although she was polite, her composed face hardened when she heard I'd gotten a book contract to write about my Mormon experiences. Even when we were striving to discuss less explosive topics—her daughter's recent return from a mission, another daughter's marriage, neighbors we'd once shared, my corporation's profit margins—not a moment's real recognition passed between us. I left her sadly, knowing we wouldn't see each other again.

Whereas with the "liberals," there is usually discomfort to discuss at least. If there is a theme among these diverse, other sorts of Mormons, it is that they believe their church has gotten off track, has strayed away from Joseph Smith's original teachings, which were radically experimental rather than socially conservative. The "liberals" often believe that today's General Authorities are too elderly, too isolated from real problems, too power-possessive and too intent upon padding the membership rolls through the worldwide missionary program to care about the hearts and problems of the minions. Through the means available they pressure for change: One particular group presents controversial papers about church doctrine and practices at a well-publicized annual symposium; the Mormon Women's Forum, whose mailing list numbers thirteen hundred, meets regularly to champion the cause of women holding the priesthood, and some of its members insist upon flouting an important Mormon ordinance: They "bless" their babies (the Mormon christening equivalent) at home rather than during the customary church service, where mothers and other women are forbidden to stand in the prayer circle that surrounds the honored child.

As they argue with their leaders, these Mormons remain fiercely loyal in their own ways to at least their ideal of a "true" church and, although willing to criticize among themselves, are sometimes very protective in front of nonbelievers. I am occasionally cut off from even the forward thinkers: During a recent summer when I was interviewing many Salt Lake City Mormons in preparation for writing this book, I arrived for my appointment with a well-known, "liberal" local columnist who had been very cordial over the phone upon hearing that I was collecting "Mormon anecdotes." Although I wanted no more than this from him—was looking for characteristic Mormon memories rather than anything controversial—he literally turned me out of his office upon learning that I was no longer "active" in the church. "I don't feel like remembering any stories today," he said coldly.

Some of these unconventional but peculiarly stalwart Mormons are suffering terribly. On that same trip, I sat in his basement office with my old friend Jacob, who as a young man at BYU had heard God's voice while praying aloud in his priesthood meeting and had thus inspired near-worship in the freshmen boys he supervised. He is an outspoken man who has again and again pointed it out to his bishops and other leaders whenever they have, in his eyes, misinterpreted church doctrine, and who—because of his willingness to entertain a very broad range of ideas—has found himself involved with

friends who have become extremists. He is the sort of searching and questioning member whom conforming Mormons
would label contentious—and dangerous.

In 1980, he and his wife, Elizabeth, agreed to hear out a
group of friends who claimed to have received an intensely
disturbing personal revelation: Jacob had been chosen to lead
a group of them into the wilderness, where they'd all become
polygamists. The proposal horrified Jacob but he is serious
about revelations. He organized a "prayer circle" in his home
that mirrored with disturbing exactness other sacred prayer
circles that are part of the temple ceremony, whose purpose
was to determine whether his friends' revelations truly came
from God. It was an unorthodox idea taken very far—partici-
pants even wore their sacred temple regalia, a terrible taboo
outside temple walls. When word of the forbidden ceremony
reached officials' ears, the reaction was sweeping: Jacob's and
Elizabeth's temple recommends were rescinded, Jacob was
accused of attempting to organize a cult, and he and Elizabeth
underwent years of interviews that probed into every hidden
corner of their beliefs.

The discipline was understandable on one hand: How
many churches would allow members to assign its greatest
powers to themselves at will? But on the other hand, Jacob
had truly meant well. During the "prayer circle," he had not
been impressed to lead his friends into apostasy; instead, he
had withdrawn from the project and had convinced some of
the others to withdraw as well. (A few of the instigators *did*
wander off to practice polygamy together and were excommunicated as a result. Mortal polygamy is unacceptable to modern church authorities, who seem to guard zealously the
church's well-scrubbed public image of perfectly conventional
families, and who disenfranchise polygamists despite allowing

the practice of polygamy to continue in the afterlife.)

The chastisement has left Jacob brokenhearted but unwilling to leave the church. "The church is our family," he said to me. "You don't divorce your family."

Instead, he has flung himself headlong into liberal activism. On the day when we were catching up with each other, he read aloud to me from a very long and impassioned symposium paper that he had written for the purpose of calling the General Authorities to repentance for their harshness and intractability when challenged. As he scolded the unseeing old men, his voice rose into such a wail of hurt and anger that the words themselves were lost. Behind his thick glasses his eyes were as obviously wounded as a child's.

I watch with awe the aching campaigners like my old friend, but I am no more one of them now than I was before, when I was unquestioning. You must value something highly to go to war to improve it, and I am not torn by even a half wish to be still on the inside. The personal freedoms I cherish most aren't available to me there; they aren't available to anyone.

Which is not to say that the Mormon part of my life was wasted; I see it benefit this second portion every day as it multiplies my experience with the bittersweet, that most affecting of all emotions. I find that I am nearly always feeling two things at once.

If I am still slightly haunted by the memory of misery I knew while too young to cope with it, I am now not as thrown off balance by miseries that I notice giving trouble to others; with some heartache for the depth of my experience, I know that sadness can end. If I missed out on knowing about other societies, and even my own American society during the fascinating sixties and seventies, my regret over lost decades is hand-in-hand today with the enduring wonder I feel as I continue to discover the world. And would I value whatever self-approval I feel if I hadn't lived so long without it?

Most of all, I have an ear (and more) trained to detect the hollow moan of dogma wherever it arises, which is nearly everywhere. When I'm up against a wall and someone or something is telling me there's only one solution, I know the message is wrong with something besides my mind; my heart, my stomach, my bowels all begin to pull me toward a larger perspective.

I can feel the lie.